D1479265

The Bells of Memory

Memory

A Palestinian Boyhood in Jerusalem

The Bells of Memory

Memory

A Palestinian Boyhood in Jerusalem

ISSA J. BOULLATA

Copyright © 2014, Issa J. Boullata

All rights reserved. No part of this book may be reproduced, for any reason, by any means, without the permission of the publisher.

Cover design: Debbie Geltner
Book design and typesetting: WildElement.ca
Author photo: David Boullata

Library and Archives Canada Cataloguing in Publication

Boullata, Issa J., 1929-, author
        The bells of memory : a Palestinian boyhood in Jerusalem / Issa J. Boullata.

Issued in print and electronic formats.
ISBN 978-1-927535-39-4 (pbk.).--ISBN 978-1-927535-40-0 (html).--
ISBN 978-1-927535-42-4 (html).--ISBN 978-1-927535-43-1 (pdf)

        1. Boullata, Issa J., 1929- --Childhood and youth. 2. Palestinian Arabs--Jerusalem--Biography. 3. Jerusalem--Biography. 4. Palestine--History--1917-1948. 5. Palestinian Canadians--Biography. I. Title.

DS109.93.B678 2014   956.94'4204092   C2013-907837-1
                                                        C2013-907838-X

Printed and bound in Canada by Marquis Book Printing.

Legal Deposit, National Library and Archives Canada
et Dépôt légal, Bibliothèque et archives nationales du Québec.

Linda Leith Publishing acknowledges the support of the Canada Council for the Arts and of SODEC.

Linda Leith Publishing
P.O. Box 322, Station Victoria
Westmount, Quebec H3Z 2V8 Canada
www.lindaleith.com

CONTENTS

PREFACE

In recent years, I have published some articles containing autobiographical elements of my life as a Palestinian growing up in Jerusalem.[*] After these, I wrote a few more articles but I did not publish them, and they covered other aspects of my life as a boy growing up in the Holy City. Now an octogenarian living away from my beloved hometown for over forty years and seeing that it is still glowing in my memory as if I were currently living in it, I thought of putting together my writings about it and about my boyhood in it. This book is the result, and it is presented to the interested reader with all the simplicity with which its parts were originally written. Some chapters in the book are longer than others or have a different mood; together they present a picture of the boy I was in the 1930s and 1940s and tell of some of the events I witnessed and the people whose life paths crossed mine. All speak of the city I have loved infinitely and will love to the end of my days.

Issa J. Boullata
Montreal

---

[*]   See Notes on p. 86.

I.   ROOTS IN JERUSALEM

I am deeply rooted in Jerusalem.

I don't mean by this to refer to my roots in the ancient Land of Canaan, and especially in the Canaanite tribe of the Jebusites who were the original Semitic inhabitants of Uru-Salem, also known as Jebus and now as al-Quds in Arabic and Jerusalem in English. Yet my family name is a constant reminder of such roots. In the middle 1940s, the Dominican linguist of Semitic languages, Father Augustine Marmarji (1881-1963) of the École Biblique et Archéologique in Jerusalem told me that Boullata was a Canaanite name; and this was later confirmed to me independently in the early 1970s by Dr. Marvin H. Pope (1916-1997), professor of Semitic languages and literatures at Yale University in New Haven, Connecticut, when he volunteered the same information on first meeting me there.

No, I am not referring to this rootedness in ancient history, important and real as it is; for the Canaanites inhabited my country since about 3000 B.C., before the Hebrews invaded them in about 1000 B.C. The descendants of the Canaanites later became the majority of present-day Christian and Muslim Arabs of Palestine, following the Arab Islamic conquest of the country in the seventh century AD and the consequent immigration into it of many Arab tribes from Arabia who settled in it and intermarried with the local people and eventually Arabized them. I am rather referring to the fact that I am personally rooted in Jerusalem because of my own life experiences and my own memories, and because of my family lore that has been part of my culture and identity since childhood.

My grandfather, Issa Hanna Boullata, had died in 1927 before

I was born in Jerusalem in 1929; but his memory lived on in his wife, my grandmother Irene, whom I knew until she died in 1936. His memory and hers lived on also in their children: my paternal uncles and aunts and, of course, my father Joseph Issa Boullata, their youngest child. Of the many stories about my grandfather that they told and others confirmed was that he was a master mason who, in the late nineteenth century and in the early twentieth century, built monumental edifices still standing in the Old City of Jerusalem, notably the colossal school of Mar Mitri next to the Greek Orthodox convent as well as the shopping complex of Dabbaghah next to the Church of the Holy Sepulchre. The latter, also known as Suq Ephtimios, is a centre consisting of one hundred and fifty-two shops intersected by cobbled public roads. It has several gateways, the most ornate of which is the triple archway nearest to the Church of the Holy Sepulchre. In the middle of this shopping complex is a circular waterworks construction with marble basins in several tiers which, at one time, used to be a beautiful and refreshing sight when the fountain operated. I have never seen it operating but, as a child, I liked to go around it to look with intent pleasure at the low glass stalls under awnings that surrounded it. These were the stalls of the Bukhara mystics of the Naqshbandi Order in Jerusalem, who sold trinkets of all kinds for a living and often sharpened knives, scissors, and axes on rotating spark-producing grindstones that always fascinated children. As a little boy, I used to buy marbles and spinning tops from them; and as an adolescent, razor blades, penknives, and other inexpensive needs.

Above the shops, on the west side of the complex, was St. John's Hospice which used to house Christian pilgrims to the Holy Land in earlier times. After 1948, rooms in it were rented to Palestinian refugees at a low rent charged by the Orthodox Patriarchate of Jerusalem, which owned the complex as a church trust, among many other properties it still holds in Jerusalem and the rest of Palestine.

After 1967, as Jewish settler groups established and expanded their settlements in the West Bank and the Gaza Strip, they turned their attention in the early 1980s to the Old City of Jerusalem. In April of 1990, the Ateret Cohanim settler group occupied St. John's Hospice, claiming the property was sold to them by an Armenian tenant via a Panamanian company, as the Jerusalem Post reported on April 17, 1990. A physical confrontation resulted when the Greek Orthodox Patriarch and his supporters tried in vain to evict the settlers and retake control of the hospice, and in the hands of the Israeli courts the matter has led nowhere. Not only is the formerly playful fountain of my grandfather silent today, but the stalls of the Bukhara mystics are gone, and St. John's Hospice continues to be forcibly occupied. My grandfather's progeny, namely, my paternal uncles and aunts, and their families and descendants as well as my father's, are now dispersed in various parts of the globe as a result of the Arab-Israeli hostilities and the creation of Israel in 1948: some still live in the Old City of Jerusalem, others in Ramallah and Amman, and others in Lebanon, Europe, the US, Canada, and elsewhere.

My maternal grandfather, Ibrahim Atallah, died in 1948 and was the last person to be buried in the Orthodox cemetery in the Nabi Dawood neighbourhood (Mount Zion) which, after the Arab-Israeli military hostilities of 1948, fell in the Israeli-controlled section of the new city of Jerusalem. His grave was therefore not accessible to his progeny living in the Old City, in the West Bank, and in Jordan. I knew my maternal grandfather well and learned many things from him, although I did not know his wife, my grandmother Latifeh, who had died during the First World War, long before I was born. Her memory and his, however, lived on in their children: my maternal uncles and aunts and, of course, my mother Barbara Ibrahim Atallah.

Why my grandfather was named Ibrahim is part of the family

lore that has been transmitted to his progeny and is still alive. It is reported that his mother could not conceive and was advised to make a trip to al-Khalil (Hebron) and go around the oak tree of Ibrahim (Abraham) there seven times and say certain prayers. So off she went on a donkey to al-Khalil with her husband and performed the circumambulation, saying the prayers. And lo and behold, she became pregnant a short time later and gave birth to a baby boy she named Ibrahim, in honour of Ibrahim al-Khalil (Abraham, the Friend [of God]), and he was to be the only child she bore. As an adult, he continued to have friends in al-Khalil whom he and his descendants cherished and visited, the town and its people still retaining a special place in their hearts.

My maternal grandfather was a reputable goldsmith and had a workshop in the Old City of Jerusalem. Having an adventurous attitude, he was one of the first Jerusalemites around the turn of the century to buy a plot of land outside the Old City walls in the region later to be called Upper Baq'a in the southwest of Jerusalem. He built himself a hut there in a virtually empty space, with hardly any neighbours, and later developed it into a simple stone house with a red-tile roof. He rode his donkey to and from his workshop in the Old City daily, a trip of about one hour. He would later see the area he invested in become a flourishing middle-class residential Arab neighbourhood with beautifully-designed modern stone houses and gardens in the 1920s and 1930s, served by regular bus lines that connected it with the rest of the city. Other similar residential Arab neighbourhoods were simultaneously growing in Jerusalem outside the Old City walls in other directions, such as Lower Baq'a, Qatamon, Talibiyya, and Thawri in the south and southwest; Sa'd-wa-Sa'id, Bab al-Sahira, Wadi al-Jawz, and Shaykh Jarrah in the north; in addition to commercial and residential areas in Shamma'a, Mamillah, Musrara, and Jaffa Road in the west and northwest.

In the mid-1930s, my grandfather decided on the advice of his now grown children to expand and modernize his home in Upper Baqʿa. He was then retired but kept all his dear goldsmith tools and equipment at home in a shack in the garden and sometimes used them to make or repair jewellery items for family members – free of charge, of course. I was a little boy when the foundations of my grandfather's new home were dug, down to bedrock. As the foundation concrete was being poured, my grandfather went to his tool shack and returned with his best steel anvil. With tears in his eyes, he threw it into the foundation as a treasured token contribution for good luck and for basic strength, with his future generations in mind. After the roof was finished amid the chorus of workers' jubilant songs, a symbolic green tree branch topped the graceful new building three floors high, now enclosing his old home and several apartments; and the workers, family members and their friends were invited to a celebratory lunch of labaniyyah, rice cooked with buttermilk and chunks of meat. My grandfather's home was now big enough for his two grown sons and their families and his two unmarried daughters to live in, in addition to apartments he rented. I liked to visit my grandfather's beautiful home as a boy, listen to his stories, and play with my cousins.

In the spring of 1948, however, my grandfather and his family became refugees in Bethlehem, living in crowded, rented quarters, having hurriedly abandoned their home and fled in fear the scene of fighting in Jerusalem between Palestinian Arabs and Zionists that would lead to the establishment of Israel at the end of the British Mandate on May 15, 1948. As he got off the car in Bethlehem, he ominously said, "The dust of my grave is calling me." He died broken-hearted several weeks later and was taken to be buried in the Orthodox cemetery in Jerusalem. His home, almost visible on a clear day from Bethlehem, was occupied by new Jewish immigrants, and his future generations were deprived of it, anvil and all.

Since 1968 I have been living far from Jerusalem, first in Hartford, Connecticut, in the United States, where I was Professor of Arabic and Islamic Studies at Hartford Seminary, and then in Montreal, where I was Professor of Arabic Literature and Qur'anic Studies at McGill University from 1975. I retired in 1999, then continued post-retirement teaching until 2004 and now, as Emeritus Professor, I continue to live in Montreal with my family. Much as I love the land I immigrated to, in which I was received with hospitality and achieved success and prosperity, for all of which I am really grateful, I feel I am still deeply rooted in Jerusalem and will continue to be so to the end of my life.

II.   THE LADY TEACHERS

"Good morning, children," Sitt Alexandra said as she stood on the landing at the top of the long external flight of stairs leading to the classrooms behind her on the second floor. *Sitt* is colloquial Arabic for *sayyida* or lady and precedes a proper name like Ms. in English.

"Good morning," the boys and girls responded in unison, arranged in four parallel straight lines in the schoolyard below, as they raised their eyes to their headmistress above.

When silence reigned, she said, "Al-Fatiha."

Prompted thus, the children recited aloud and together the Opening chapter of the Qur'an, in clear Arabic and with a measure of rhythmic intonation:

"In the name of God, the Compassionate, the Merciful. Praise be to God, Lord of the worlds, the Compassionate, the Merciful, the Master of the Day of Judgment. Thee only do we worship, and Thee alone do we implore for help. Guide us in the straight path, the path of those on whom Thou hast bestowed blessings, not those who have incurred wrath, nor those who have gone astray."

It was my first day at school in the autumn of 1934, and I had been looking forward to it all summer. I did not know what to expect. All I desired was to learn how to read and write like the adults. Yet here I was, listening to beautiful Arabic words I had not heard before, which I could not recite with the other children because I did not know them by heart, as they did. So I listened, and I realized that the words were a prayer to God different from the prayer I had been taught by my parents at home and had repeated silently at the beginning and end of every day:

7

"Our Father, who art in Heaven, hallowed be Thy name. Thy kingdom come, Thy will be done on earth as it is in Heaven. Give us this day our daily bread, and forgive us our trespasses as we forgive those who trespass against us. And lead us not into temptation, but deliver us from evil. For Thine is the kingdom, the power, and the glory for ever and ever."

After the recitation of Al-Fatiha, the headmistress gestured to the children to climb the stairs and go to their classrooms. They were no more than sixty boys and girls, and each class was led in turn and in an orderly fashion by its homeroom mistress. I walked behind my new classmates until I reached a room which, I learned later, was called Kindergarten, as the sign on its door said in Arabic. And I liked it at first sight, not only because my teacher was the headmistress herself, Sitt Alexandra, with her good looks and friendly smile, but also because the room's walls had big colourful pictures of animals and birds, and its large windows let in abundant light that made everyone cheerful. One of its windows opened on to a lovely garden behind the schoolhouse at the same level as the school's backdoor, which did not have stairs like those of the front door leading down to the schoolyard.

I do not remember now what I learned on that first day of my first academic year, but I remember it was a happy day and I did not want it to end. Yet it ended with the ringing of a bell, from which I understood that my day was portioned into times for learning, times for rest and play, and times to eat or go home. On the next day, I came early to school, eager to continue my contact with a new place which had brought me great happiness and in which I had begun to absorb new knowledge in a most pleasant way and to win new friends in play and study.

This first day was later followed by many more, until school became an intimate and inseparable part of my life. I began to greet the headmistress with my schoolmates in the collective manner in the schoolyard every morning and to recite Al-Fatiha with them by heart before climbing the stairs and going to my kindergarten. And I began to vie with my classmates in acquiring knowledge and attracting the attention of my teacher, to ally myself with some of them against others to achieve advantage in play, and to do other things that were natural signs of a normal merging in my new society.

Called the Thawri Elementary School for Boys and Girls, it was located on the top of the mountain in the middle of the Thawri neighbourhood , commonly called Tori or Abu Tor in colloquial speech. Situated in the southern part of Jerusalem and separated from the walled Old City by a hill and by a valley leading eastward to the village of Silwan, this Arab residential neighbourhood had modern buildings and its inhabitants were mostly Muslims. My father had moved our family there from Upper Baq'a, a modern Arab residential neighbourhood inhabited mainly by Christians and situated in the southwestern part of Jerusalem. He considered our home there too far from the only government school in the area, the Thawri School; so he decided to move from it and rent an apartment for our family that would be closer to the school, to which I and later my younger siblings went.

The school consisted of four classes: the kindergarten and three elementary classes; the four classes were housed in rooms on the second floor around a hall, which also had a teachers' powder room and a small kitchen where the teachers could make tea or coffee and warm up their lunch. Since the school building was constructed on an incline, the first floor below had only two large rooms: one was used as a refectory for pupils who brought their lunch with them, and the other as a storage room. The latter room was commonly called "The Mice House" and was reputed to be the dreary place to which badly behaving pupils were temporarily consigned for punishment, although I never saw either pupils or mice in it. The schoolyard was not too large but sufficiently comfortable for the

9

small student body to play in. It had a wall of rough, un-cemented stones on three sides, a wooden gate for the pupils' entrance, two huge and shady trees, and separate lavatories for boys and girls at the far end. Behind the school on the opposite side of this yard was the lovely garden visible from the kindergarten room, but it was for the pleasure of the staff only. It too was enclosed by a wall on three sides, it had a small fountain and pond in the middle, several footpaths and flower beds, a number of shady trees and benches, and a gate at the far end.

The school had four lady teachers: Sitt Alexandra, the head-mistress and kindergarten homeroom teacher and Sitt Nigar, Sitt Asma, and Sitt Wasila, each of whom was responsible for one of the three elementary classes. The pupils were mostly Muslim; as for the teachers, Sitt Alexandra and Sitt Wasila were Christian, and Sitt Nigar and Sitt Asma were Muslim. The teachers had all been trained professionally at the Teachers' Training College in Ramallah and had acquired the latest teaching and pedagogic methods of modern education offered there by the Department of Education of the British Mandate of Palestine.

My kindergarten year was a pleasant introduction to my later academic formation. I do not remember its details but I know that, by playful instruction, I came to learn how to read, how to add and subtract, how to draw and write in pencil, how to make figures in plastic dough, and how to sing a few songs with my classmates.

Among the many stories that Sitt Alexandra told us in class, I remember one about a little boy who ate unripe green apples from the garden tree at his home against his mother's advice, and he became ill and had pain in his stomach. He cried, "aaa" and "uuu" and "iii"! To imitate him, the class was asked to say, "aaa" and "uuu" and "iii". The children obliged willingly and rather gleefully, and were asked to repeat the three sounds several times. Then the teacher showed them three cards, with one letter written on each, and they were the three long vowels of Arabic: a (as in fat), u (as in food), and i (as in feet). "These letters are called 'Letters of illness' in Arabic," she explained, referring to the little boy's stomach pain which, we were told, was cured on drinking a cup of chamomile tea prescribed by his mother. Showing one card at a time, Sitt Alexandra then said, "This is a, aaa... and this is u, uuu... and this is i, iii." The pupils were asked to write them in the air with their index fingers by imitating their shapes in turn, and to say their sounds aloud, which they did with alacrity. Then she asked the class to guess the one card she showed, while hiding the other two, alternating between the one shown and the two hidden. Then she asked them to write the three letters in pencil on a piece of paper. By the end of the hour, and despite the deceptive semblance of chaos, the children had learned how to read and write the three long vowels of Arabic, correctly called "letters of illness" in Arabic grammar books, as I later learned. The three cards were then returned to their proper pockets in a cloth board hanging on the wall and containing pockets for each of the other letters of the Arabic alphabet, which we would learn later.

Addition and subtraction were taught on an abacus, which stood on a large wooden frame in front of the class. Counting was first taught by sliding the abacus beads, one bead at a time, on the horizontal wires within the upper frame of the abacus; there were ten rows, and each row had ten beads, every five of which were of the same colour, but different in colour from the next or previous five. After several weeks, when the names of the numbers from one to one hundred had been mastered orally, addition or subtraction were taught for several more weeks. The first row of ten beads visibly showed the results of adding or subtracting by sliding the beads to one side or the other. The next rows were later used to learn addition and subtraction to include numbers up to one hundred. Learning to write the numbers followed several weeks later; more complicated processes like multiplication and division were left to the higher elementary classes.

This was serious learning in kindergarten, but it was absorbed by us children in play and was conveyed to us by pleasant methods. There was also fun for fun's sake, like drawing with crayons, playing with plastic dough to make invented figures, and singing rhymes and ditties, acting some of the latter with movements of the hands, fingers, and arms to represent – for example – the swimming of fish, the flying of birds, the turning of the wheel, and the clapping of children at play, in one particular song. Unconsciously this fun was also a learning process and an acculturation to school discipline and common social living. There was also time for complete silence and rest when we children laid our heads on the little table at which each of us sat, pillowing our heads on our folded arms and closing our eyes for a nap, which was especially blissful on hot afternoons.

A few weeks into the kindergarten year, I was given the privilege of entering school from the teachers' entrance at the back of the garden behind the schoolhouse. On entering, I was told I had to walk on the side lane and directly down the side stairs leading to the schoolyard, in order to join my schoolmates there and later climb the front stairs with them to our classrooms when it was time for school to begin. I was not to wander or tarry in the garden. I was pleased at being given this privilege because our home was nearer to this garden entrance and, by using it instead of going around to the main entrance, my way to school was shortened. Walking on the side lane of the garden, I dared to look at the beautiful flowers, smell the air redolent of their scents, and listen to the birds chirping and the water gurgling as it fell into the pond from the fountain. These were unforgettable moments of ephemeral private pleasure in a paradise with no occupants. I enjoyed this short walk daily until, one day, I caught sight of a whitish grey trunk of a tree that I had not seen earlier, standing immediately to the right of the garden entrance as I came in. I was struck with fear and quickened my steps.

The whitish grey trunk was that of a dead tree. It had no branches and no leaves. It was a hollow trunk, yet it was standing firmly. It was bulky and ugly, towering and forbidding. At its foot was a rugged opening, arched like a gate. And within was empty darkness...

I was afraid that a little goblin would come out of it at any moment and shout at me for disturbing his master, who was trying to sleep in his little underworld kingdom down below. I hurried on my way and did not look back.

My father, who was the best storyteller I ever knew, had one evening told my siblings and me the story of a poor woodcutter who cut wood from forest trees for a living. He sold the wood he cut and bought food for his wife and children, but he could not always provide them with all they needed. He complained of his poor life conditions but always hoped he would have better circumstances in the future. One day he went farther than usual to cut wood in an area of the forest where he had never been, where he saw a lovely tree with abundant thick branches. He rolled up his sleeves, sharpened his ax on a small whetstone he carried with him, and began cutting chunks from the nearest branch. After some time, he heard a voice chiding him. Looking around to find from where the voice came, he saw a little goblin at the foot of the tree, on the side opposite the one he was working on. Dressed as a military guard with a little sword at his side, the goblin shouted at the woodcutter, "You are hitting and hitting this tree with your ax and causing such a loud noise. My master down below is trying to sleep and you are giving him no chance. You had better stop the noise or I will call the other guards, and we will stop you by force."

"I'm sorry," the surprised woodcutter said as he stopped cutting wood, "but I'm trying to make a living and feed my wife and children. Who is your master, anyway?"

"He is the king of the underworld, and his kingdom is just below this tree. I will now take you to him so that you may explain to him your problem and why you were causing all this noise. Please follow me."

The goblin then entered through a little opening arched like a gate at the foot of the tree, and the woodcutter followed him, surprised at first that his large body could easily fit into the little opening, but later feeling comfortable as he descended a long flight of well-lit stairs leading to a majestic hall. There were little candelabras hanging from the ceiling, and their lights were reflected on the marble floor. In the front of the hall was a little golden throne, but it was empty, and in the hall were courtiers, lovely little ladies and gentlemen in stately clothes, waiting for the king to arrive.

When the king arrived with his pages, everybody stood up until the king sat on his throne and gestured to everyone to sit down.

"There has been a lot of noise, and I could not sleep," he said. "Now tell me, what's the matter and who is this man?"

"He's a woodcutter, Your Majesty," said the little goblin guard. "He was trying to cut wood from your tree above, and I stopped him."

"Well done, guard. Come forward, woodcutter."

The woodcutter stepped forward in awe and explained, "I was simply trying to make a living by cutting wood in order to sell it, and buy food for my wife and children, Your Majesty."

"You seem to be a good and honest man," the king said. "What would you say if I were to relieve you of woodcutting and make you a rich man?"

"But I'm a woodcutter, Your Majesty. However, I don't mind

being a rich man."

"Fine. Take this purse of gold coins," the king said. "This will be your capital. Use it to start a lumber business in your country. But don't ever come again here to my country in order to cut wood from my tree and disturb my kingdom."

And so the woodcutter left and eventually became a rich businessman dealing in lumber, and his wife and children lived with him happily ever after.

"But I am not a woodcutter and do not want to become a lumber businessman: I want nothing to do with the little goblin and his king," I said to myself every time I warily passed by the whitish grey trunk of the hollow tree until, when the little goblin never appeared to me, I was finally reassured that I would be left alone.

The three school years after kindergarten were as pleasant and educational as my kindergarten year at the Thawri School, and my knowledge continued to develop incrementally. I learned to read Arabic well, using the graded series of *Al-Jadid,* the popular and extensively used four reading books by the great Palestinian educator and author Khalil Sakakini (1878-1953). First published in Jerusalem in succession between 1924 and 1933, they were used in government schools all over Palestine as well as in some other Arab countries, and were reprinted many times.

Right from the first page of Book One in kindergarten, I learned to read the words *ras* and *rus* (meaning "head" and "heads," as the illustration showed), and on the second page *dar* and *dur* (meaning "house" and "houses" as the illustration also showed) using an additional letter to those learned earlier, and so on to the end of the book, which culminated in teaching the Arabic alphabet from reading the names of illustrations of everyday things seen

15

and experienced by the pupils, rather than learning it abstractly as single letters arrayed in a specific order. Book Two in the next class introduced simple sentences and easy grammatical structures, using daily conversation. Books Three and Four in the following two classes offered further simple readings and brief stories, without the insipid rules of traditional grammars.

I also learned to write Arabic well, and my handwriting was particularly neat and beautiful using the graded calligraphy workbook series of calligrapher Mustafa al-Shihabi, with a model top line by him on each page to be imitated. I also learned the four processes of arithmetic, some basic data of geography and history, and important information on hygiene and cleanliness. Above all, I learned to be a good member of a small society and an example to my younger siblings, who joined the school in later years.

One of the important things I learned was to use my hands to make beautiful and useful things. At the beginning it was making figures with plastic play dough in kindergarten. My imagination was given free rein to make what I liked and, to go by what my mistress Sitt Alexandra told my parents, I was so creative that I made things the other pupils never thought of, such as spoons and forks and kitchen utensils; but I also made figures of animals, birds, and people in different professions. Using wax crayons, I also created pictures of children playing, a boy flying a paper kite, and other scenes; in later years, when we used coloured pencils, I drew more detailed pictures after I quickly finished drawing anything that the mistress had prescribed, like a pitcher or a glass or any single model object she brought before the class that I deemed too easy or unimaginative. In the higher elementary classes, I also learned to knit and to embroider in the crafts hour. My project one year was to knit a woollen scarf, and I was proud to wear it later on. I embroidered a cushion cover, which I gave to my mother to use at home, and I made a wicker wastepaper basket with a round, thin plywood bottom and sides made of woven rattan. This last project was the most complicated and was undertaken in the third elementary class under the supervision of Sitt Wasila, who helped me in making equidistant holes on the circumference of the round plywood bottom for the rattan stems to be rooted in, and provided me with the rattan shoots after having soaked them in water to make them pliable to weave around the stems and build up the basket sides. I used this wastepaper basket at home for many years.

However, what I remember most vividly from my childhood days at the Thawri School for Boys and Girls, is that it was there that I read my first book from cover to cover in one sitting. The book was an Arabic book entitled *Al-Dajaja al-Saghira al-Hamra'* (*The Little Red Hen*). I was about eight years old. The joy I felt during the weekly hour in Sitt Wasila's class devoted to silent reading of Arabic books that she distributed to her pupils was ineffable and is still with me to this day. Little did I know then that that was the opening for me to the endless world of literature.

I could easily read and enjoy *Al-Dajaja al-Saghira al-Hamra'* in the third elementary class and, later in the same class, many other similarly delightful books in the weekly silent hour of Sitt Wasila's class. But imagine my great surprise and delight, one day, on seeing the author of my Arabic reader, Khalil Sakakini himself, in my classroom. He was paying an official visit to my school as the government's Inspector of Arabic. He was a strongly-built man, tall and portly and awe-inspiring. He wore a red fez and had a commanding and dignified presence. His eyes shone brilliantly with intelligence, an encouraging smile never abandoned his lips, and he spoke in classical Arabic.

Sitt Wasila asked me to read a new text to him. I read it aloud, trying to conceal my nervousness and slight intimidation. When I finished, he asked for the meaning of the word *fawran* in the text. No one in the class knew, so he used the word in a sentence and asked again for its meaning. I raised my hand with a few other students, but he did not call on any of us. He used the word *fawran* in another sentence and asked for its meaning again. More students now raised their hands to answer. But he did not call on any of them until he gave a third sentence using the same word again. At that moment, almost all the students raised their hands eager to answer, and those asked said, correctly, that it meant "immediately."

I admired Khalil Sakakini and wanted to be like him when I grew up, a good teacher and educator with an excellent knowledge of Arabic language and literature. I later learned much more about him. He was the author of more than a dozen books, and he had been an indomitable figure whose participation in Palestinian politics in Ottoman and British times often led to his imprisonment. He always cherished freedom and dignity and truth and justice as essential human values worth struggling for. He had a good sense of humour, was interested in music and singing, played the violin, and liked good food and a hearty life enhanced by physical exercise and sports. As a young man he had emigrated to the US but returned to live in his beloved homeland. At different times of his life, he was a member of a variety of literary circles in Jerusalem, which brought the best Arab intellectuals and writers of the day together for informal conversations, which were a pleasure to attend. He had friends among the writers of other parts of the Arab world and was in contact with them; and he was elected as a member of the prestigious Academy of the Arabic Language in Cairo.

I later read his books, and particularly liked two very personal books: *Sari*, in which he gathered all the letters he had sent from Jerusalem to his son Sari who was at university in the US between 1931 and 1935; and *Li-Dhikraki (In Your Memory)*, in which he poured out his heart at the death of his beloved wife Sultana in 1940, for whom he had written his best poetry. While many Arabs would rather keep such personal feelings and thoughts private,

Khalil Sakakini made his public, strongly believing that the best literature is written about the genuine inner experiences of a human being, expressed beautifully to display their impact on him and to wonder at the meaning of life. Another book of his that I liked was *Kadha Ana Ya Dunya* (*Such Am I, O World*) a memoir edited by his daughter Hala that was published posthumously in 1955. In this book, he opened himself to be fully known as he passed through life, recording his various experiences, his thoughts, and his feelings without reservation. The book is not only a frank register of his life but also of Palestine, its society, its people, and its intellectuals, and is written as if consciously addressed to history so that all may know the point of view of the uniquely untraditional person he was, who always yearned courageously and outspokenly for something new and better, and disliked being bound by conventions. "Such am I, O world," he told history, using the very words of the heroic and ebullient classical Arab poet he liked most, Abu al-Tayyib al-Mutanabbi (915-965).

In the 1948 *Nakba*, he lost to the Zionist fighters his home in Qatamon, one of the most beautiful residential Arab neighbourhoods of Jerusalem outside the Old City. His belongings were savagely plundered and his library barbarously looted, and he and his family had to flee for their lives and take refuge in Cairo. I briefly saw him afterwards in the Old City of Jerusalem, which had come under Jordan's rule after the rest of Jerusalem and much of Palestine had come under that of Israel, following the 1948 war at the end of the British Mandate. A fallen titan, a broken old man, his dignity still bristled; the shine in his eyes had dimmed a little, but he still believed that justice would eventually prevail and truth would always triumph. The streak in his thinking that had begun in the latter part of his life to favour the poetry and thought of the pessimistic and skeptic classical Arab poet Abu al-'Ala' al-Ma'arri (973-1058) had become stronger in him. He died in 1953.

19

III.   TURBULENT TIMES

I don't remember much about my first childhood home in Upper Baq'a in the modern part of Jerusalem. It was a rented apartment on the ground floor of a building with three floors, in the topmost of which lived the owner, noted Jerusalem lawyer Henry Catan, and his family. Upper Baq'a, like Lower Baq'a to the west, was a beautiful residential neighbourhood of middle-class Arabs, mostly Christians. It was developed by Arabs who had left the crowded residences in the Old City of Jerusalem, mostly in the 1920s and 1930s, and built modern stone houses with gardens.

My childhood was a happy one at this home. We had a front yard with trees, and my siblings and I played there with the neighbourhood children. My maternal grandfather Ibrahim Atallah and his offspring, my aunts and uncles, lived nearby with their children, my cousins, so we could see them and play with them. However, my paternal uncles, the Boullatas, lived in the Old City of Jerusalem, so their children were farther away. On occasion we took the half-hour bus ride from Upper Baq'a to Jaffa Gate and then walked to their homes through the alleys of the Old City enclosed within its Ottoman city walls. My paternal aunts lived in other parts of the city or the country with their husbands, and their children were even farther away, so we met them only rarely, on feast days and other special occasions.

I remember my second childhood home better than my first because I was older when we moved to it in 1934, when I was about five years old. It was a rented apartment on the ground floor of a four-apartment building with two floors, and was owned by

Shaykh 'Abd al-Bari Barakat. It was in the al-Thawri neighbourhood, an Arab residential quarter mostly owned and inhabited by
middle-class Muslims. It was nearer than Upper Baq'a to the Old
City to the south, and was separated from it by a hill and a valley leading to the village of Silwan. My home in the al-Thawri
neighbourhood was near its western entrance and stood on a side
street off the neighbourhood's main road, which branched off from
Bethlehem Road at the intersection where the Government Printing Press stood, next to the Jerusalem Railway Station. East of the
building in which my home was, a large adjacent mansion rose with
a beautiful garden. We children knew this only as Mr. Bowman's
house, but later in life, I learned that Mr. Humphrey E. Bowman,
the British director of Palestine's Department of Education from
1920 to 1936, lived there with his family and a staff of genteel servants. No wonder adults always spoke of that mansion with awe
and admiration.

From the doorstep of my home I could see, across the valley,
parts of the Old City of Jerusalem to the north that were not hidden by the intervening hill, Mount Zion, on which stood Prophet
David's neighbourhood, al-Nabi Dawood, one of the oldest Arab
neighbourhoods outside the city walls of Jerusalem. Across the valley I could see Jaffa Gate, known in Arabic as Bab al-Khalil (Hebron
Gate) because it leads to the city of al-Khalil (Hebron) to the south,
past the town of Bethlehem; it also leads to Yafa (Jaffa) to the
west, past the town of Ramleh, hence its name Jaffa Gate in English. From my home I could also see, across the valley, the al-Aqsa
Mosque and its dome in the southeastern corner of the Old City
and, within its city walls, and looking west, I could see the building
of the Government Printing Press across Bethlehem Road, opposite the entrance to our neighbourhood.

There was a treeless open space in front of our home, across the
unpaved side street from our front door. Although one section of

this open space was a little higher than the rest, it was level enough for us children to play on, even for an occasional informal soccer game in which the standards of Association football (i.e., soccer) were not necessarily kept; the size of the field was small, the goal posts were piles of stones on opposite sides, the demarcation white lines of the field were nonexistent, and the two teams often had fewer than eleven players each.

From this home it was only a few minutes' walk uphill to my school. It was in fact its closeness to school that motivated my father to move us here from Upper Baq'a. But this home was still far from my father's place of work, the Telegraph Office, which was located in the General Post Office building on Jaffa Road in the heart of the main business area of the modern city of Jerusalem. He usually had to take a bus to work and then walk for a short distance. This home was next door to that of one of my paternal aunts; her youngest son, my cousin William, sometimes played with us children, although he was a little older than any of us. He was mostly the referee of our soccer games and the mediator of our occasional petty quarrels.

Our home was an apartment consisting of four rooms around a central hall, and it had a short corridor in the back leading to the kitchen and bathroom. If to my father "a man's house is his castle," to my mother "home is where the heart is." My father was the one who provided in love all we needed and did his best to protect and guide us, and my mother was the one who kept our home a pleasant place to live in – with her love, her constant attention to the delicious and nutritious food we ate, the smart and clean clothes we wore, and the gleaming and spotless accommodations we had, thanks to her continuous labour. Both parents were genuinely interested in what we children did, and both cared conscientiously for our upbringing in the good traditions of the family, Arab customs and mores, and the Christian faith.

I was the firstborn of their six children. With a couple of years between each of their children and the following one, my sister Renée was next to me, then my brother André, then my brother Jamil, and then my sister Suʿad. My youngest brother Kamal was yet to be born in 1942, several years following my younger sister, after we had moved to the Old City of Jerusalem in 1938 – to my third childhood home, or to what I should rather call my boyhood home. Ours was a close-knit family with strong bonds of love between all of its members, but as a result of the Palestine tragedy, we are today far apart from one another and far from our beloved Jerusalem. Renée passed away in 2012 in Bethesda, Maryland, USA. My other siblings are alive and well: André and Jamil live in London, England, with their families; Suʿad and her husband live in Bethesda, Maryland; and Kamal and his wife lived in Menton, France for many years and now live in Berlin, Germany. I live in Montreal, Quebec, Canada with my family. My father died in Jerusalem in 1960 and my mother in Washington, DC, in 1984.

The years during which we lived in the al-Thawri neighbourhood were turbulent years in Palestine. Not that the years before or after were peaceful. In the Balfour Declaration of 1917, the British government had promised to view with favour "the establishment in Palestine of a national home for the Jewish people." The Arab population of the country, which constituted the majority of its inhabitants, was in opposition to this and, in 1922, to having its principles and aims incorporated into the League of Nations' charter of the British Mandate for Palestine. The Palestinian people expressed their opposition in repeated petitions, memoranda, and delegations of protest, and then in occasional street demonstrations and later in violent uprisings. I was a baby of six months when the 1929 uprising simultaneously exploded in August in Jerusalem, Hebron, Safad, and other parts of Palestine, killing many Jews as well as many Arabs. The 1930s had a more intense and urgent character to their turbulence. Adolf Hitler had come to power in Nazi Germany, and greater numbers of Jews than ever before immigrated to Palestine to escape the horror and inhumanity of his anti-Jewish policies. Although still smaller in number than the Arab population, the Jewish population was growing and acquiring Palestinian lands and properties, threatening to become the eventual masters of the country with the support of the British Mandate as per the charter of the League of Nations.

My parents tried to shield us from any feelings of insecurity at home. And although, as children in the 1930s, my siblings and I understood little of what was really going on, we sensed something was amiss. The truth was that there was an Arab armed rebellion in the country against the British Mandate. Arab rebels occasionally roamed the streets of our neighbourhood with their weapons, especially in the dark of night; the British army was more visible in the country with now larger numbers, ominous weaponry, and armoured cars; and the Palestine police force under the organization of the British mandatory government was more alert to new civic duties of public security, crowd control, and people's movements. The Arab turbulence came to a head in the Rebellion of 1936-1939, which spread all over Palestine, beginning in April 1936 with a general strike that paralyzed the country for six months.

During the strike, all Arab shops were closed, all Arab buses and trucks stopped running, all Arab workers refrained from unloading shipments of imports and loading cargoes for export, and all Arab trade came to a standstill. The Palestinians demanded that the British suspend Jewish immigration and begin negotiations to form a national government for Palestine. The trains, however, continued to run because they were under the administration of the British Mandatory government, and all Arab employees of the government – like my father – continued to fulfill their work obligations lest they lose their jobs to Jewish employees, but they privately contributed a percentage of their salaries to the strike fund and national resistance. My father had to go five miles on foot to perform his daily duties at the Telegraph Office, my school teachers at the government school continued their usual teaching and I my usual learning; but the atmosphere everywhere was tense.

Meanwhile, my mother had to provide food for the family, and provisions were running low – mainly rice, bulgur, lentils, beans, chickpeas, flour, olive oil, ghee, salt, onions, garlic, pickled olives, cheese, sugar, tea, coffee, and other storable commodities like canned sardines and corned beef. Once in a while, a butcher appeared in our neighbourhood, slaughtered a sheep clandestinely deep in Karm Karimeh, a grove of olive trees on the incline by the main road next to our home, hung the carcass on a tree, and was swarmed by neighbours wanting to buy fresh meat; he had to finish his business quickly before he was discovered by the roving members of the "national committees" who enforced the strike.

Women from the villages surrounding Jerusalem appeared from time to time carrying on their heads baskets loaded with fruits and vegetables that they had grown but could not take to sell at the closed markets. They brought them furtively to the doorstep of buyers in our neighbourhood and elsewhere to sell, though fearing their goods might be mashed underfoot by the strike enforcers, if they were discovered. Similarly, village women went around to the homes to sell the milk and butter of their cows or goats. My mother, like all the neighbours, took advantage of all these opportunities during the six-month strike and kept her family well fed. No member of our family ever missed a hearty meal or went hungry to bed.

The strike lasted until October 1936, longer than any other general strike in the Middle East or Europe. Instead of responding to the demands of the strikers and suspending Jewish immigration, the British announced a new quota for additional Jewish immigrants, and this inflamed Arab passions. Sporadic violence started in

May of 1936 and increased over the summer months despite severe British punishments. Small Palestinian guerrilla bands fought with the British army, sabotaging a number of government buildings and railways. The Lebanese guerrilla leader Fawzi al-Qawuqji entered Palestine in August 1936 and headed groups of Arab rebels in the area of Nablus and Jenin. The Arab Higher Committee, formed in April 1936 by Palestinian politicians and headed by the Mufti, al-Hajj Amin al-Husayni, realized that the general strike was not achieving its ends and was rather benefiting the Jewish community economically and hurting the Palestinians; they decided therefore to accept an appeal from the kings of the Arab countries to end the strike; and so the strike ended in the hope that the Arab kings would, as promised, intervene with Britain and help persuade the British to modify their policies in Palestine.

The British government sent to Palestine a six-man commission headed by Lord Robert Peel to study the situation. They interviewed Palestinian and Zionist leaders and British officials for a few months after their arrival in November 1936 and issued their report in July 1937. They recommended the partition of Palestine: a Jewish state would be created in much of the coastal area and in Galilee, with a suggestion that Jewish immigration would be limited to twelve thousand annually for five years; and a Palestinian state would be created in the rest of Palestine (excluding a zone to remain under the British Mandate consisting of Jerusalem and Bethlehem with a corridor to Jaffa, plus an enclave containing Nazareth), with a provision that the Palestinian state would be joined to Transjordan and ruled by Emir Abdallah.

The Peel Commission's report served only to anger the Palestinians and make them resume their rebellion with more violence, including the assassination of some British officials and of Arab persons perceived to be collaborators with them. The government outlawed the Arab Higher Committee and its local committees and rounded up those Palestinian leaders it could lay its hands on. Al-Hajj Amin al-Husayni escaped to Lebanon, some of his colleagues were deported, and others who had left Palestine were forbidden from returning. The rebellion intensified, and local and regional guerrilla leaders took control of the national movement under the continuing leadership of al-Hajj Amin from exile. Abd al-Qadir al-Husayni, son of the former leader of the Palestinian national movement Musa Kazim Pasha al-Husayni (who had died in 1934), was the guerrilla commander of the Jerusalem region and other areas.

At the height of the rebellion, the Old City of Jerusalem was totally in the hands of the rebels for five days in October 1938 until the British forces took it back after fierce fighting with the rebels in its alleys and lanes. From my home in al-Thawri, I could see small British reconnaissance airplanes repeatedly flying over the Old City of Jerusalem pinpointing the centres of rebel resistance in it by sending down signals of silver flashes that descended like shooting stars to direct and guide the British forces on the ground in the maze of the old city.

As a nine-year-old boy, I did not realize the significance of what was happening, but I was becoming increasingly aware of the political and military developments, which were the main conversation topics of the adults I listened to as well as the talk among my friends at school. One day I saw a fully-armed, lone Palestinian rebel lurk behind a hillock right across the road from our front door and open fire on the guards of the Government Printing Press next to the Jerusalem Railway Station. The exchange of fire lasted for almost half an hour, while my mother made us children hide away from the windows in the back corridor, despite my curiosity to witness the exciting event. When the shooting stopped, I looked, but the rebel had gone, leaving a pile of empty bullet shells on the ground.

Soon afterwards, there was a house search by British soldiers in our neighbourhood. It was not the first, nor would it be the last, and they were all conducted without a court warrant. A number of armed British soldiers entered our home and went into every room, opening wardrobes and drawers, emptying their contents on the floor and rummaging through them; they overturned furniture and fumbled mattresses and pillows, looking for hidden arms and ammunition. In the kitchen they ransacked my mother's provisions, pouring out her neatly organized supplies and mixing their contents. They asked a few questions in slang English mixed with broken Arabic about what we had seen, then left to continue their house search elsewhere. The government had made a new law that allowed them to demolish a home in which arms were discovered or ammunition was found, and to arrest its tenant. We children were afraid at the sight of armed soldiers in our home, but my mother was not, or pretended she was not – perhaps to give us reassurance.

My father was away at work most of the times we had house searches. But one time, he was shaving in the morning before going to work, and the British soldiers took him away in his pajamas with other neighbourhood men; they did not let him continue shaving or even wipe the shaving cream foam off his face. With the other men, he was taken to the parking lot of the nearby Government Printing Press where they were all subjected to an investigation. While each man was being interrogated separately by a British officer sitting at a table, an informant hidden in the back of a canvas-covered, British military truck was watching through a hole in the canvas and giving an agreed-upon clink to signal whether the person interrogated was a rebel sympathizer or was in any way connected with the national rebellion. In the end, a few men were detained for further investigation and the others were let go, including my father, who related to us what had happened when he returned home; he then continued his shaving, and went to work, about two hours late.

I don't remember the time when I came to know that my father owned a handgun that he hid at home – an unlicensed Belgian pistol with a few rounds he had purchased on the black market. Like many other Palestinians during the national rebellion and later, he felt safer at home with a pistol at hand. When I was an adult, he told me that he hid it in the restroom, concealed in the toilet flush-tank, which was out of order and so always unused and empty; high up on the wall behind our old-fashioned toilet seat, the tank was of the kind that had a chain you had to pull down in order to flush the toilet. My father was later afraid to keep his pistol there, when house searches by the British soldiers became more frequent and more rigorous, so he hid it in a specially-made wooden box he buried under the floor tiles in the far corner of the drawing room. The weapon and its hiding place at home were kept secret from us children lest we divulge the fact to others, either innocently or boastfully, and British ears would hear.

The British authorities often had to impose curfews in Jerusalem and other parts of Palestine in order to restrict rebel movements and bring the country under their control. My father, like other government officials, was given a curfew pass and an identity card that permitted him to go to his office and come back home during curfew hours. He had to walk because no cars or buses were permitted to move during a curfew, and he often did that in the dark of night, and as a lone walker he was stopped several times on his way by British patrols examining his papers.

When there was no curfew, British soldiers at many checkpoints in the city stopped and frisked people. They were particularly suspicious of men who wore the Arab headdress, that is, the head kerchief and black rope (the *kufiyya* and '*iqal*); for this headdress was what the rebels wore, and the British aimed at isolating them, limiting their movements among the population, and eventually catching them. It was at this juncture that the leaders of the national movement issued orders that all Palestinian men should wear the Arab headdress to confuse the British. My father, like many civilian Arabs in the city, used to wear a red fez; now he and all Palestinian men took to wearing the Arab headdress. This made his solitary walk to and from work during curfews, especially in the dark, all the more problematic, and he had to keep his curfew pass and identity card in his hand to show to British soldiers screaming at him to halt or be shot.

The Palestinian rebellion persisted in the face of British punitive measures, and the rebels, despite limited means, inflicted many casualties on the British and suffered many themselves in turn. Though they succeeded in derailing government trains, burning government buildings, cutting telephone and telegraph lines, and disrupting government operations, they did not however succeed in defeating British purposes. One of their tactics was to sprinkle sharp little nails on the main highways in Palestine to stop or delay British military traffic. Even in Jerusalem, long stretches of road were often covered with nails which had to be swept away before military vehicles could pass. British soldiers often compelled Arab civilian passersby to sweep the nails away with their bare hands; my father and I were caught up in this kind of forced labour a couple of times when we were unwittingly walking about Jerusalem on one errand or another.

The Palestinian rebellion subsided a little when the British, having realized that partition of the country was unfeasible, called for a Round Table Conference in London, at which they met separately with Zionist leaders and Arab delegates from Palestine, Iraq, Transjordan, Saudi Arabia, Yemen, and Egypt. Then, in May 1939, the British issued a White Paper which suggested that Palestine would become independent in ten years as a unitary state if Palestinians and Zionists agreed, that land purchases by Jews in Palestine would be restricted, and that Jewish immigration to the country would have to be approved by Palestinians after a five-year quota of fifteen thousand annually was filled. The White Paper was a victory of sorts for the Palestinians, but it was rejected by the Arabs as well as the Zionists. The outbreak of the Second World War in September 1939 deferred the problem; and the establishment of Israel in 1948 after the UN Partition Plan of November 1947 created new complications.

My parents did their best to let me and my siblings have a relatively happy and normal life at home in spite of the political turmoil. Every Christmas my father put up a lovely Christmas tree, a fragrant fresh pine, which he himself decorated with colourful glass balls, feathery artificial birds, tiny bells, paper angels, small candles, and silver tinsel, with a big star on top. Every evening of the Twelve Days of Christmas, he made us children line up in front of the tree and sing in Arabic "O Christmas tree" (*Shujayratun*), while he accompanied us on his banjo; sometimes we also sang for visitors.

My mother baked all kinds of goodies and traditional chicken dishes for Christmas. On New Year's Eve, she always cooked a cock which, to our amazement and amusement, crowed at mealtime before being carved and served – my father helping it, with his napkin covering his mouth! The other dishes had to be white, usually including stuffed *kubbeh* balls with yoghurt sauce, in order to inaugurate a "white" and happy new year. The New Year's Eve meal began with a small drink of red wine from a common glass: in descending order of age, each member of the family drank the wine, then shook the glass, at the bottom of which was my father's gold ring that caused a festive clink. After each member of the family drank, he or she exclaimed, "*Zito!*" (Life!), to wish everyone a good life and golden opportunities in the new year. We spent a big part of the night playing games.

31

In the early morning of New Year's Day, we woke up at the sound of a knock on the door by the man delivering the large, round tray of hot *kunafa* that my father had ordered the day before. We began our new year by sitting around the round tray and avidly eating a breakfast of this sweet pastry together so that our new year would also be "sweet." For New Year, my mother spruced up our home and decorated the lintel of every inner door in our apartment with narcissus and tangerines clinging to their green leaves, in a wish for an auspiciously flourishing and "green" new year.

At Easter, to celebrate Christ's resurrection, my mother made us coloured boiled eggs and sweet semolina cookies in the shapes of the crown of thorns and of the sponge soaked in vinegar associated with Christ's crucifixion and death on the cross. She traditionally cooked a spring lamb stuffed with rice, pine seeds, and spices; this was served after a traditional lamb soup containing spicy meatballs and parsley, and made with a mixture of well-beaten, fresh, and spiced eggs that made the soup whitish – and delicious.

Attendance of church services at Christmas and Easter was an experience we enjoyed: we had to go to the Old City, to St. James Cathedral, our parish church, and to the nearby Church of the Holy Sepulchre, which was crowded with people from various parts of the world. In the Old City, we had occasion to see our Boullata cousins, whom we did not see often, and to visit their families, who gave us coloured hard-boiled eggs at Easter. We often cracked eggs with our cousins in a contest to see whose egg had the strongest shell. In the usual contest, the winner whose egg did not break could take all the broken eggs. We did not play to win with our cousins, but we did play to win with children who were not related to us.

During his annual leave, my father took the whole family on holiday. This was usually in summer, and we often went to Jaffa, stayed at a hotel, spent most of our day on the beach, and swam

ISSA J. BOULLATA

in the Mediterranean; we also made occasional visits from Jaffa to nearby Tel Aviv and spent time on its lovely beaches. It was exciting for me to see the sea for the first time, but it was no less exhilarating to see it again and again annually and to swim in it, we being Jerusalemites living in a mountain city. We went also to Haifa, which was farther from Jerusalem. We enjoyed seeing the ships in the port of Haifa, and we realized how the view of the Mediterranean from Mount Carmel was even more breathtaking than from Jaffa and actually matchless.

In the summer of 1938, my father took us to Egypt by train, and we stayed mostly in Cairo. This was the farthest trip from home that I made in my childhood. We had first to go west to Lydda and then change trains to go south to Egypt, crossing the Suez Canal. It was exciting for me to see another Arab country, to notice the different Arabic dialect of its people, to ride a tram for the first time in my life, and to marvel at the people in Cairo who seemed not to go to sleep at night. It was also exciting to see the great Nile flowing gently and majestically through Cairo and giving life to all Egypt. The internationally renowned Cairo zoo was the most amusing part of the trip for us children, the Pyramids and the Sphinx at Giza were impressive sights, and the Museum of Egyptian Antiquities in Cairo was memorable for its amazing artifacts from different periods of ancient Egyptian history. The most spectacular relics there for me were those of Tutankhamen, recently popularized as King Tut, the pharaoh who became ruler of Egypt when he was nine and died at the age of nineteen, and whose tomb was discovered only in 1922, almost intact after more than three thousand years with its wealth of historical artifacts.

As a boy of about nine, I did not understand much of what I saw then, but what I saw was the basis of the knowledge on which I built much more, in later years, when I visited Egypt several times as an adult. The more important thing was that the world to me

33

then was beginning to be so big, so multifaceted, and so diverse and interesting that I have ever since remained open-minded to it and aware of the benefits of seeing it. There was so much to learn about the world from my travels. As a result of this realization, I think, I eventually made several trips over the years to countries of the Arab world and Europe, as well as within the US and Canada after my emigration from Palestine in 1968. This apart from five later trips around the world by air in the 1990s, during which I visited some countries of the Far East, including Hong Kong, Indonesia, Malaysia, and Singapore, and some countries of Europe, including Germany, France, Switzerland, Spain, Italy, and the United Kingdom.

IV.   THE BOOKWORM

In 1938, when I completed the third elementary class, which was the highest in my elementary school at al-Thawri, my father did not want me to continue my education in the free government school system of Palestine. He himself had gone to al-Dusturiyya School, a private secular elementary school in Jerusalem established in 1909 by Khalil Sakakini, where he learned Arabic, Turkish, history, and arithmetic, and then to the Collège des Frères.

This is where my father now sent me to complete my schooling. Collège des Frères was a private high school in the Old City of Jerusalem established in 1876 and run by the Christian Brothers, an internationally Catholic teaching order, who were helped by a number of non-clerical teachers. The school charged high fees, but my father wanted me to have the advantage at it of learning French and English in addition to Arabic, and of benefiting from its distinguished curriculum and possibly from its famous discipline – although it was not noted for its sports activities.

The change to a boys' school with male teachers after my earlier schooling at a co-educational school with female teachers was a little disrupting, but I quickly adapted myself to it, despite the daily attendance at Mass and catechism classes that were compulsory for Christian students of all denominations; the Muslim students and the few Jews were exempted. The school day was longer and fully occupied with intensive courses, except for a mid-morning break and a mid-afternoon break of fifteen minutes each and a lunch break of one hour.

What I missed greatly was the silent hour we had had at al-

35

Thawri school with Sitt Wasila's interesting and colourful picture books. My new school had a library, but it consisted of locked glass bookcases hung along one wall in the long second-floor corridor in three sections: Arabic, English, and French. There was no catalogue, not even a list of books, and they never seemed to increase in number. The Brother responsible for the library unlocked one of its bookcases for a few minutes once a week and gave the eager students who cared to come and swarm around him what he selected for them to borrow and read.

I was usually the first to arrive at the Arabic section. After several years, I thus came to read many of the Arabic books of Kamel Kilani for children and young adults, mostly graded and simplified books in large print and with pictures, based on selected (and expurgated) stories from *The One Thousand and One Nights* and on other Arabic classics, but also adventure stories adapted from Western literatures like Daniel Defoe's *Robinson Crusoe,* Jonathan Swift's *Gulliver's Travels,* Robert Louis Stevenson's *Treasure Island,* and Miguel de Cervantes's *Don Quixote.* Noticing I was an avid and rather more advanced reader, Frère Épiphane, the Lebanese Brother responsible for the Arabic bookcases, slipped to me more than one book per week. When I was in my early teens, he selected for me Arabic historical novels to read; especially those of Jurji Zaydan (1861-1914), all twenty-two of them, which I enjoyed because they taught me Arab history while entertaining my inquisitive mind. Arab history was deficient in the school's curriculum, and so was geography. Pretty soon, I had read the books the school 'library' had to offer, and I needed richer and more satisfying reading, which is when I was lucky enough to fall upon a treasure trove at home.

This was a collection of Arabic books and magazines that had belonged to my father in the 1920s and 1930s and that were kept in a crate under a couch. As a younger man, freer of family and work responsibilities, he read widely in his leisure time. Now overworked and latterly bedridden with rheumatoid arthritis, he had little interest in reading, but he gladly let me read his collection and he took pleasure in discussing my readings with him. To me, this was even better than Sitt Wasila's reading hour. I was now, in the mid-1940s, blossoming intellectually, and my father was a very knowledgeable guide and a most loving mentor. To him I owe a great measure of my literary orientation.

Prominent in the collection were some of the books of Jubran Khalil Jubran (1883-1931), of whom my father was an admirer. His *The Prophet* (1923), rendered into Arabic as *Al-Nabi* by Archimandrite Antonios Bashir, who died in 1966, was my introduction to Jubran's contemplative romantic thought and lyrical style, which immediately charmed me. This charm was further reinforced by reading his *Dam'a wa Ibtisama* (*A Tear and a Smile*, 1914), *Al-Arwah al-Mutamarrida* (*Spirits Rebellious*, 1908), and *Al-Bada'i' wa al-Tara'if* (*Wonders and Curiosities*, 1923). Fascinated by Jubran's poetic prose style and by his rebellion against social conventions and his defence of the downtrodden, I later read all his works wherever I found them, and I even pursued the works of all his Arab colleagues in the Pen Bond of New York, of which he was the leader.

Another book in my father's collection was *Al-'Abarat* (*Tears*, 1915) by Mustafa Lutfi al-Manfaluti (1879-1924), a collection of sad stories he adapted from Western literature. An Azhar graduate, he clung to a traditional prose style which oddly conveyed a melancholy romantic mood bordering on sentimental pessimism. I later read more of his books elsewhere, including *Al-Nazarat*, his three-volume book of essays, and the novels he adapted from French: *Fi Sabil al-Taj* (*Pour la Couronne* by François Coppée), *Al-Fadila* (*Paul et Virginie* by Bernardin de Saint-Pierre), and *Tahta Zilal al-Zayzafun* (*Sous les Tilleuls,* by Alphonse Karr), and the retold play *Al-Sha'ir* (*Cyrano de Bergerac*, by Edmond Rostand), but I did not take to al-Manfaluti and his style.

My father's collection included two novels by Anatole France (1844-1924): *Thaïs* and *Le Lys Rouge,* translated into Arabic by Muhammad al-Sawi Muhammad as *Tayis* and *Al-Zanbaqa al-Hamra'* respectively. Even in the Arabic translation, the pure and limpid language of this 1921 Nobel laureate and master of literary style came through. I liked him and later read in French some of his other books including his *Le Crime de Sylvestre Bonnard;* I admired his satiric tone and delicate irony, and I learned from him what a subtle and powerful tool language can be.

Not so was the style of another book in my father's collection, *Les Amants de Venise* by Michel Zevaco, translated into Arabic as *'Ushshaq Finisiya* by someone whose name I don't even remember. Nor so was the style of another translated novel on Pope Alexander VI (Rodrigo Borgia) telling about his political and ecclesiastical intrigues and his many mistresses and children. Although I appreciated the fact that he patronized great artists like Raphael and Michelangelo, I don't think he ever made me forgive his misuse of office, but rather made me ever wary of people in high positions.

Books of a totally different nature in my father's collection had a great influence on my thinking; they were by Salama Musa (1887-1958), the Egyptian liberal thinker and modernizer who, while studying in England, had adopted the socialist philosophy of the Fabian Society and propounded it in his Arabic writings. Of his other writings, I read his book *Nazariyyat al-Tatawwur wa Asl al-Insan,* popularizing Darwin's theory of evolution, and I have ever since supported this theory and concurred with its more recent scientific developments; likewise, I have supported Salama Musa's feminist views and his call for an Arabic literature of free ideas and simple style addressed to the common people, not to the elite. I later enjoyed reading his autobiography, *Tarbiyat Salama Musa,* and learning from it the course of his intellectual development.

The Arabic magazines in my father's collection were incomplete series of well-known monthlies, most of which dealt with topics similar to the ones mentioned above. They included Jurji Zaydan's *Al-Hilal* , which was historical, literary, and general – and was later edited by his sons Emile and Shukri Zaydan; Ya'qub Sarruf and Faris Nimr's, *Al-Muqtataf*, which was scientific, industrial, agricultural, and general; Mary Yanni's feminist, literary, and general magazine *Minerva*; and *Al-Nafa'is al-'Asriyya*, in which the Jerusalemite Khalil Baidas (1875-1949) published fiction and literary translations, especially from the Russian. *Al-Riyada al-Badaniyya* specialized in medical information and health, and it included sexology, in which, as a teenager, I was extremely interested. These and other magazines opened up intellectual horizons for me on Arab writers from Egypt, Lebanon, Syria, Iraq, and Palestine. I was certain the Christian Brothers at my school would not approve of my readings, but I did not let the thought deter me.

When my father's crate of books had nothing more to offer me, I came to know a much larger 'crate' that contained over 100,000 books and periodicals. That was the library of the YMCA. I was in my last three years of secondary school in 1944-1947 when I joined the Y, more eager than ever to read and have social contact with a wider world. The Christian Brothers forbade their Catholic students to join this Protestant institution, but since I was an Orthodox Christian, I felt I was free to join it and I did, despite my school's discouragement. I never regretted this act, for in addition to athletics at the Y, I made new friends, and a new world opened up for me in the public lectures, art exhibits, documentary films, musical concerts, and occasional plays I could attend there. No one ever tried to make me a Protestant at the Y, as was propagated at my school.

Unlike the YMCAs in some other parts of the world, where the institution specifically caters to the poorer classes, the Jerusalem Y, which had been established in 1933, was a bustling centre of social, intellectual, and athletic activities. Its new building was dedicated by British General Edmund Lord Allenby*, who travelled from England to speak at the well-attended opening ceremony. Its unusual and beautiful architectural style was designed by Arthur Loomis Harmon, architect of the Empire State Building in New York. It has been described as "a sermon in stone, rich in symbolism representing the three monotheistic faiths." The monumental building had a graceful high tower in the middle and was flanked by two domes, under one of which was a large auditorium with a stage; a modern gymnasium was under the other, with a swimming pool in the basement. At the foot of the tower was a wide terrace that overlooked trees and a lovely garden, and there was a large soccer pitch with bleachers behind it. This was a landmark building in Jerusalem on Julian's Way opposite the majestic King David Hotel.

Once inside the Y, one felt the plush atmosphere of the place with its modern furniture and shining, spanking cleanliness. It had a good hostel, a cafeteria with a soda fountain, comfortable lounges, a lecture hall, a boys' department, and an evening school, and its tower had a carillon that was played on festive occasions, notably by the Arab Jerusalemite musician Salvatore 'Arnita.

The library had a large reading room with tables and chairs surrounded by comfortable leather armchairs; in this reading room were a card catalogue, stands for current newspapers and periodicals, and shelves with reference books and encyclopedias. Its large collection of books was kept in an inner space behind the reception desk, where a librarian was always ready to fetch the books whose catalogue numbers you gave him or her. This was a library different from the 'library' of the Christian Brothers' school and the crate collection of my father. Since Jerusalem had no public libraries, this was my first experience of a real library, and it was here that I continued to form myself intellectually. Here I continued to read the monthlies *Al-Hilal* and *Al-Muqtataf*, which my father's collection had introduced me to, but now I also read other literary journals like Albert Adib's then-new Lebanese monthly *Al-Adib*, the older Egyptian publications *Al-Risala*, edited by Ahmad Hasan al-Zayyat, and Ahmad Amin's *Al-Thaqafa*, as well as a newer one, Taha Hussein's *Al-Katib al-Misri*, and others.

I read more books by authors my father's collection had introduced me to, and I discovered many more, including writers in English I began to admire like Ernest Hemingway, John Steinbeck, H. G. Wells, Graham Greene, and Aldous Huxley. I discovered Marcel Proust, André Gide, and André Maurois. And it was in this Protestant institution's library that I first came to use *The Catholic Encyclopedia* and *The Encyclopaedia of Islam,* of whose existence I had not even known.

The courses I took with Jabra Ibrahim Jabra (1920-1994), who was my teacher of English literature at school and a member of the YMCA, where he established the Jerusalem Arts Club after returning from Cambridge in 1943, gave me ideas on what to read in English; similarly, the courses I took with Mounah Khouri (1918-1996), who taught me Arabic literature at school and was also a member of the Y (and later Professor of Arabic Literature at the University of California at Berkeley) suggested what I might read in Arabic. Both teachers helped in forming my literary sensibility and in introducing me to contemporary authors. They became my friends, and both eventually came to be well-known published writers. I later wrote several articles in Arabic and in English about their literary contributions, for they were both creative writers and poets. I owe them much of my literary orientation and I have honoured them both in separate Festschrifts.

V. THE OLD CITY

The home in which my family and I lived in the late 1930s and the 1940s was a small house in the Old City of Jerusalem. It was located in the Christian Quarter within the city walls, in an alley in the Jaffa Gate neighbourhood, and it was the property of the Coptic Church of Jerusalem. To one side was a house that was the property of the Armenian Church of Jerusalem that was inhabited by an Armenian family; to the other was a large multi-family house that was the property of the Franciscans of Terra Sancta. They owned many houses in the city, which they let only to members of the Catholic community of Jerusalem, known in Arabic as *Latin* and they charged them no rent. This latter house was inhabited by four Arab Jerusalemite families who were *Latin*.

The houses in our neighbourhood, as throughout the Old City, were connected with each other so that one could virtually go from one rooftop to the next. Narrow alleys between houses on opposite sides snaked through the city leading to main streets, to other neighbourhoods, and to rows of shops that constituted the various markets and the special-commodity *suqs* – the spice market, the greengrocers' bazaar, the butchers' market, the smiths' market, the coppersmiths' market, and the cotton merchants' market. Each house, however, had its own front door and accommodated one family and often more, depending on its size. Despite a variety of traditional architectural designs, each house had an open, central courtyard accessed through the front door, and around it the apartment rooms for family living. A flight of stairs on one side of the courtyard led to an upper floor in some houses. The apartment rooms in the upper floor looked out on the upper and lower courtyards and might also have windows that looked onto the alley.

Like other houses in the Old City, our house had a well in the ground floor courtyard; this well collected the rainwater that fell on the domed roof and was channeled through pipes and ducts. Water for daily use had to be drawn from the well with a bucket because there was no running water in the apartment rooms. We bathed in a tub, heating water on a kerosene stove and pouring it from a small container. In the courtyard, there was a privy for the use of all the house residents. In most houses in the Old City, the privy consisted of a single hole in the floor over which one squatted. A few houses – like ours – did replace this with a toilet bowl and seat. Kerosene lamps and candles provided lighting until electricity became available for city streets and alleys. Room heating in the cold winter months depended mostly on movable braziers in which fine charcoal glowed silently, but these were replaced in affluent homes by movable, tall kerosene stoves with a wick, and sometimes by gas stoves.

Our home was rented from the Coptic Church by a Greek man who was originally from Cyprus, a grocer named Costa Michaelidis, who was also the owner of a tavern on the main street, just outside our alley. He had lived in the house for many years with his Athenian wife, Anna. Since they were childless and the house was too large for the two of them, Costa sublet out the larger rooms on the upper floor to my father, keeping the other rooms for himself and his wife. A few years after we moved to this house in 1938, Anna died, and Costa followed her a short time later. My father now rented the whole house directly from the Coptic Church and, for a couple of years, sublet the unused rooms to tenants who paid him their rent. However, our family was growing and had increased with the birth of my youngest brother, Kamal, in 1942, so my father decided to make use of the whole house to accommodate his family. It was then, with the whole house at his disposal, that my father provided it with electric wiring and lighting – and at his sole expense, because the Coptic landlord did not wish to bear the costs. And it was then that our family had its first radio and, a little later, its first refrigerator. By this time, I had completed my high school studies at the Collège des Frères, and I could now begin to forget all the years when I had done my homework by the dim light of a kerosene lamp.

Despite the lack of some modern amenities, living in our Old City home was pleasant, and my parents made a great effort to make it happy and productive. For one thing, our home was close to our schools. My two sisters went to the girls' school of the Sisters of St. Joseph, almost next door, at the entrance of our alley; and my brothers and I went to the Collège des Frères, which we reached by going to the nearby main street and up the hill past the Casa Nova, toward the New Gate area, just a ten minute walk. My father's place of work at the General Post Office on Jaffa Road outside the Old City was no more than a twenty-minute walk from nearby Jaffa Gate. He was the one who usually went to market to purchase what we needed, sometimes taking me with him and teaching me how to choose the best vegetables and fruits at a greengrocer's, how to select them from a peasant woman's basket in the bazaar, and how to order the best cuts of meat from a hanging carcass at a butcher's. My mother was mostly responsible for home chores and, with her usual verve and exuberance, she kept it spick and span, cooked delicious foods, and saw to it that every member of her family was taken care of. She was the first one to get up in the morning and received the fresh milk delivered regularly by our young milkman or his mother, a peasant woman who had her own cows in the nearby village of Silwan. My mother prepared breakfast for us children and herself. If it was not Lent, the fast before Virgin Mary's Dormition day on the fifteenth of August or the fast before Christmas – when the Orthodox Church rules that we should abstain from dairy products – our breakfast usually consisted of bread, hot milk or tea, my mother's homemade orange marmalade, apricot or quince jam, olives she had preserved, white cheese or *labanah* (strained-yoghurt cream), sometimes scrambled or boiled eggs, and the usual Palestinian dip of *zait u za'tar* – olive oil and ground spiced thyme. My mother made Turkish coffee for my father, who hardly ever had breakfast, and then she embarked on her day's work with diligence, making the beds, sweeping and tidying the house, and preparing the other meals of the day from scratch. She also tended a small garden of potted flowers and plants in the upper courtyard, in addition to a potted bitter orange tree.

As a girl, my mother had gone to Mrs. Thompson School, a private Protestant missionary school in Jerusalem, where she learned Arabic, English, arithmetic, and religion, and then on to the Don Bosco Salesian Sisters School where she had learned art and many handicrafts. She knitted sweaters for everyone, made embroidered cushions, crocheted doilies, sewed clothing for her children, and even made her own dresses. Furthermore, she did the cooking, darned socks and stockings, did the ironing, and always kept members of her family well-dressed, neat, and presentable and her home in tip-top shape. On festive occasions, she spruced up the house, used lace bedcovers that she had hand-made herself, and offered particularly sumptuous meals. She also entertained visitors in the reception room, offering them coffee, home-baked cookies, and chocolates.

On the first floor of our house, as one entered the front door and walked to the courtyard, there were three rooms and the privy: one room was without windows, the second had a window looking on the courtyard, and the third had a small aperture partly obstructed by the stairs that led to the second floor. That is why these rooms were mostly used for storage, including an alcove screened by a fixed wooden partition with a door, where my brother Kamal kept hundreds of comic books. Costa had used some of these rooms as a warehouse to store his supplies of grocery goods and his tavern's backup barrels of spirits, and his wife Anna used one of them as a kitchen. In the courtyard of the first floor, there was also a stone platform in which was the mouth of our well, which was noted for its cool and fresh water, thanks to the scrupulous attention that my father – and Costa before him – paid to the absolute cleanliness of the roof, letting the earliest rains of the winter season cleanse it first and run off into the city drainage before directing the movable water spouts into the well.

For a couple of years, when my father first started being the leaser of the house, he let the unused first-floor rooms at a very low rent during Holy Week to poor and pious Coptic pilgrims who came to Jerusalem from Egypt to celebrate with others from all over the world the greatest Christian event of the city's history, namely, the death and resurrection of Jesus Christ. They could not afford even cheap hotels or inns, so my father provided one or two of these families with bedding, but they were responsible for their own meals. Other homes in the Old City did likewise for Copts, Cypriots, and other poor pilgrims. The presence of the Coptic guests in our house was educational for us children, helping us to understand not only their colloquial Egyptian dialect of Arabic but also something about their customs, especially their piety and their strict keeping of Lent by fully abstaining from meat and dairy products until Easter Sunday.

The second floor of our home consisted of four domed rooms with doors opening onto the upper courtyard. The largest of these rooms had a fixed wooden partition in it, creating a smaller section that was used as a pantry and a larger section that was the children's bedroom; this also had a table we used for study and doing homework. This room had an inner door leading to the master

46

bedroom, which also had an inner door leading to the dining room which, in turn, had an inner door leading to the reception room. At the back of this last were two beds, where we older boys slept, so that we were separate, for the sake of modesty, from our sisters and younger brothers.

The kitchen on the upper floor was independent of these interconnected rooms and appeared to have been an afterthought of the builder and a recent addition to the upper courtyard. In relation to the other rooms that formed a sort of crescent facing east, the kitchen was like a star between the crescent's two points. Built of brick, and with a comparatively low roof of red tiles, the kitchen was small with two little windows. It contained a table on which my mother could cook on a small kerosene stove of the gas-producing type called *primus*. This table had an inbuilt sheet-metal covering with raised edges that formed a dishwashing area that could be drained through a corner pipe into a container that had to be emptied periodically into a drain in the upper courtyard linked to the city drainage system. Next to this table was a small oven with four legs on a stand; this could be heated by a small kerosene stove placed underneath. The kitchen also contained a stand with a washbasin. Hung from the wall over it was the *musluk,* a small water tank with a spigot, and above it on the wall was fastened a framed mirror. The *musluk* was used to wash one's hands and face, and the mirror helped when shaving.

The small tank had to be constantly refilled with water from a large, nearby metal drum that contained water that had to be hauled in five-gallon tin cans from the well and up the stairs. The chores of hauling water were divided among the able and willing members of our family, but my father in the end hired a man to do the job and fill the metal drum in the kitchen at regular intervals. At one time, he entertained the idea of installing a pump and water pipes to bring the well-water upstairs more easily, but the project was too complex and was never realized. My mother washed clothes by hand in a tub, usually on the floor in the upper courtyard near the kitchen, helped by one or both of my sisters when available; she, too, in the end hired a washerwoman to do the job in the lower courtyard. The clothes were hung to dry in the sun on the roof, which was accessed by a fixed wooden flight of stairs at the back of our upper courtyard.

The roof was made of stone and had domes of different sizes, the biggest being the one over the children's bedroom and the pantry; we children eventually learned to climb it by running up it and not by creeping. The area of the roof was protected by a wall and was sometimes used as a place of recreation or for a picnic in the sun in the early days of spring after the long cold winters. From our roof, we had a panoramic view of the Old City of Jerusalem dominated by the two domes of the Church of the Holy Sepulchre — the Dome of the Resurrection and the smaller Dome of the World's Centre next to it. In the distance we could see the two domes of al-Haram al-Sharif — the Dome of the Rock and the smaller Dome of al-Aqsa Mosque — beyond which, to the east and outside the city wall, rose the Mount of Olives topped by the elegant steeple of the Church of the Ascension. After my family left this house, it became the Convent of the Virgin Lady for Coptic Nuns.

To live in the Old City of Jerusalem surrounded by its historic Ottoman wall with seven gates was exciting and different from living in the modern city outside the wall. As I was growing up, I was determined to explore as much of my Old City as I could, gradually getting to know its different neighbourhoods, its markets, its churches and mosques, its physical configurations — and its people. Motorized traffic connecting it to the modern city was limited to a couple of wide, main streets, and these were macadamized but had no sidewalks. One had to go on foot through the Old City's cobbled alleys and markets, trying to avoid laden donkeys and camels, porters carrying heavy burdens of crates of goods on their backs tightly tied by ropes to their heads, or carriers transporting dripping water-skins or large carcasses of animals from the slaughterhouse. The city authorities in time replaced the cobbles of the alleys and markets with flagstones or concrete paving, which made walking easier, but walkers still jostled in crowded areas. The marketplaces were noisy during the daytime, with carriers alerting passersby to make way, vendors hawking their wares, often in poetic terms when describing fresh fruits and vegetables, newspaper sellers announcing the day's headlines, and radios in shops and coffeehouses blaring a newscast or favourite Arabic songs. Apart from this din, I used to like to listen to the melodious voice of a blind man or another begging for alms on the side of the street in the marketplace, chanting a passage from the Holy Qur'an in eloquent and well-articulated Arabic. At night, all was quiet in the marketplace except for some coffee houses; the shops were shuttered and their garbage was piled up in front of them for next morning's early collection; the night watchman roamed about silently, sometimes checking padlocks to ascertain they were secure. In the residential neighbourhoods, noises were subdued at night but, in the stillness, one could sometimes hear an indoor conversation, a heated debate, or even a domestic quarrel when the windows on the alley were open to let in fresh air in summertime.

The mood of the Old City of Jerusalem varied according to the religious calendar. It was bustling with Christian pilgrims and Western tourists in the springtime before Easter. The streets and alleys were crowded, the hotels were fully booked and busy, and the souvenir shops did brisk business selling their Holy Land gifts and handicrafts. The historic places along the Via Dolorosa marking Christ's painful way to crucifixion were visited, and the Church of the Holy Sepulchre teemed with overflowing crowds, particularly at the special dramatic services during Holy Week: on

49

Maundy Thursday, at the ceremony of the Washing of the Feet; on Good Friday, at the service of the Lamentations; on Saturday of the Light, at the observance of the Emanation of Light from Christ's tomb; and on Easter Sunday, at the celebration of the Feast of the Resurrection.

In addition to the crowds of pilgrims and tourists, the local Jerusalem Christians also participated in the annual Easter rituals. In one particular celebration, it was usual for the Arab Orthodox Christians on the Saturday of Light to go at noontime in a large procession through the main street in the Christian Quarter, making their way to the Church of the Holy Sepulchre. On reaching the Holy Sepulchre, they participated in the prayers in the unlit church and, in the end, they were the first to receive the light emanating from Christ's tomb at the hand of the Greek Orthodox Patriarch, which they passed on immediately to all their darkened churches in Jerusalem and elsewhere. While the huge bells of the church were pealing with resounding reverberation all over the city, it was always an exhilarating sight to see the light spread among the people at this ceremony in the Church of the Holy Sepulchre, dispelling the darkness. They would have come prepared with bundles of candles, and they took the light from one another and passed it on. Some pilgrims took this light with them in lanterns when they went back to their homelands. I liked to attend all these Easter celebrations as a boy with the multitudes of locals, pilgrims, and tourists; they helped bring meaning to my faith and religious traditions, and they infused in me a deep sense of history and a strong feeling of belonging to a universal community.

One week before Good Friday in the Holy Week of the Orthodox Church calendar, Muslims used to gather in large numbers in Jerusalem from nearby parts of Palestine, with massive contingents from Hebron and Nablus, to prepare for the celebration of the Nabi Musa Festival. They entered the Old City on different days in separate, awe-inspiring processions consisting of thousands of people, and they assembled in al-Haram al-Sharif to join the Jerusalemite Muslims who would have received them in equally awe-inspiring processions at the city gates as they arrived, each group carrying its town's *bairaq* or banner and the flag of its own Sufi group. The *bairaq* of Jerusalem was kept year-round at Dar al-Bairaq, a house in the Old City, and was unfurled to be used at this Nabi Musa occasion, often by the Mufti al-Haj Amin al-Husseini or his representative, carried by a strong man in all the processions.

After Friday prayers at al-Haram al-Sharif, they all proceeded on foot and horseback to the Muslim shrine of Prophet Moses, *al-Nabi Musa*, some twelve miles east of Jerusalem on the way to Jericho. These processions were deliberately slow in entering the city and then in leaving it, with the celebrating assemblage cheering and loudly responding to leaders' calls and chants, some of which sometimes had political anti-British overtone. Their movement forward was punctuated by dancing and by mock fencing matches in open clearings in the midst of the crowds. They returned to Jerusalem from the Nabi Musa shrine on Good Friday, after a week of prayers and camping at the site, and then dispersed following Friday prayers at al-Haram al-Sharif. After the 1936 rebellion, the British mandatory government of Palestine restricted the Jerusalem portion of this annual Muslim festival that had been celebrated by Palestinians since the thirteenth century.

In Ramadan, the ninth month of the Muslim calendar, dedicated to fasting from sunrise to sunset, Jerusalem assumed a prayerful mood. Al-Haram al-Sharif and other mosques were places for more than the five ritual prayers per day, and they received people for additional private devotions and religious readings, especially at night. Restaurants offered no food in the daytime, although some of them had a secluded section for those permitted by Islamic law to eat during the fast, such as travelers away from home. Jerusalemite Christians did not eat publicly in the presence of Muslims in consideration for their fast. There were special Ramadan pastries and sweetmeats made for sale by confectioners in the market, notably *qatayef* and *mushabbak,* which Christians and Muslims enjoyed equally, as did everyone with a sweet tooth. Apart from foodstuffs, business was slack in the marketplace, and people were generally quiet and pensive. But as sunset approached, movement quickened in the marketplace and eventually came to a virtual stop, with the streets emptying as Muslim families met in their homes to break the fast at sunset, at the sound of the Ramadan cannon and the calls from the city minarets. Later on, movement returned to the city as men frequented coffeehouses, among which some had a storyteller to entertain their clients until a late hour with customary narratives, chivalrous romances, and folk epics; the advent of television gradually put an end to this tradition.

I wish I knew the other Quarters of the Old City of Jerusalem as intimately as I came to know the Christian Quarter and the Muslim Quarter. I am sure the Jewish Quarter had its own moods also according to the religious calendar, but it was not within my circle of daily life and boyhood experience. I walked through the Jewish Quarter a number of times to see what it looked like, but mostly in its market, to buy goods of a special kind for my family, such as salted fish. The Jewish Quarter was not different from the other Quarters of the Old City of Jerusalem in layout and general medieval appearance, with its lanes and alleys, houses and shops. It had many synagogues, some of which were quite old and historic, like the Hurva Synagogue, and it had several yeshivas. On Saturdays, the Jews prayed at the Wailing Wall, the Western Wall retaining the vast platform of the ancient Temple Mount and of the contemporary al-Haram al-Sharif compound. The Wailing Wall stood east of the Jewish Quarter in the Maghariba neighbourhood, and its prayer area was an alley barely ten feet in width. That was vastly enlarged into a plaza in June 1967 with the Israeli demolition of one hundred thirty-five homes of Muslims and two historic mosques in the neighbourhood.

My life as a Palestinian Arab was focused on other things while growing up in the Jerusalem of the 1930s and 1940s, things that eventually made me what I am today, including my interest in Arabic literature and Islamic culture and my distrust of politicians — Arabs, Israelis, and others in the world — from some of whose unwise and self-interested decisions my Palestinian people and I still suffer.

VI.   COLLÈGE DES FRÈRES

Classes at the Collège des Frères were larger than I had been used to, with thirty-five or forty students in each in the early years, fewer later on. The school day was longer and the courses were more intensive. We went to school seven days a week, including Sunday when there was one class after our attendance at Mass, but there were no classes on Thursday afternoons. Most of the students were Christians of different denominations, with a few Muslims and one or two Jews.

There could be no mistaking the fact that it was a Christian institution. A crucifix hung on the front wall of every classroom, every class started with a brief prayer led by the teacher, and the school day ended with a prayer in class emphasizing contrition. Every written assignment submitted to a teacher, whatever its subject, had to have the initials "J. M. J." inscribed on the top margin of each page, referring to Jesus, Mary, and Joseph (in Arabic Y. M. Y. for Yasu', Maryam, and Yusuf), although this requirement was gradually dropped in the upper years. Attendance at Mass in the school chapel was obligatory for Christians of all denominations every morning; the few non-Christians were exempted from this. Similarly, catechism classes were compulsory for all Christians, and the non-Christians exempted; and there was no doubt the catechism intended Catholic indoctrination, to the despair and futile protest of some non-Catholics, like myself, when there was occasionally a glaring disparity between denominational beliefs.

There could be no mistaking, either, that the school was a French institution. It raised the French flag on a flagpole on top of the building. During the Ottoman rule over Palestine and until the First World War, it had close relations with the French Consul in Jerusalem who encouraged its curriculum, to advance not only French culture but also Catholicism in order to offset Anglican, Russian Orthodox, and Greek Orthodox educational influences in the country. During the British Mandate, the role of the French Consulate weakened because of the rising influence of English culture and the requirements imposed by the British Mandate's Department of Education. But the school continued to raise the French flag during the British Mandate in Palestine, although it avoided any appearance of political involvement with France or allegiance to it. When the eastern part of Jerusalem came under the suzerainty of Jordan after the British Mandate ended in 1948, the school regularly raised the Vatican's flag, and it has done the same under Israeli occupation since 1967.

At any rate, the curriculum of the school was French for a long time, in that French was the language of instruction for most courses, even under the British Mandate, whereas English and Arabic were taught only as languages. I learned to add, subtract, multiply, and divide in French, and I still use French unconsciously for all my silent calculations to this day. Furthermore, the order of the school's classes at the Collège des Frères followed that of France at the time, so that the lowest class of the school was the ninth (with two divisions, upper and lower) and the highest class was the first; and the scheduling of courses was virtually concurrent, so that Arabic – for example – was taught at the same time in the school, and students changed classrooms between periods in order to go to the classroom for their level of Arabic. When I joined the school in 1938, I was placed in the ninth class (upper division) for all my courses except Arabic, for which I was placed in the seventh class, because my Arabic was of a higher standard as determined at my brief entrance test.

It was not until 1940-41 that the order changed, and classes rose from Elementary One to Elementary Seven and then from Secondary One to Secondary Four, just like other high schools in Palestine, both private and public. I was no longer embarrassed to explain the odd system of classes in my school to my cousins and friends from other schools.

French continued to be the medium of instruction in the elementary classes until the middle 1940s, and students in the free school and sometimes in the fee-paying school continued to be prepared for the public examination of the French *Certificat d'Études Primaires*. It was not until later on that French was taught as a language only, and English became the language of instruction, especially in secondary classes, so that history, mathematics and the sciences were taught in English. Furthermore, a student had to belong to one class for all his courses and had to take them in one classroom with different teachers in successive hours, and there was no longer a system whereby a student had to move from one classroom to another for different levels of his courses.

Established by Frère Évagre in Jerusalem in 1876, with its first classes welcoming students in 1878[*], the Collège des Frères belonged to a Catholic international teaching order of Brothers founded in France in 1680-84 by a priest named Jean-Baptiste de La Salle (1651-1719), who was canonized in 1900. In the years when I was a student there, his saint's day on May 15th was celebrated jubilantly by students and teachers in the school's chapel with special French hymns and songs. Members of his order are not priests but celibate Brothers who wear a black habit with a collar having two white and starched broad flaps hanging down below the chin on the upper chest. They live a simple life of piety and are dedicated to education; they have schools around the world, many of which are free. In Palestine alone, they have had five schools: in Jerusalem, Bethlehem, Jaffa, Haifa, and Nazareth, the last of which was closed in recent years, and the one in Haifa much earlier. In Bethlehem they further established the University of Bethlehem in 1973. In addition to their schools in Palestine, the Brothers have schools in Lebanon, Egypt, and other Arab countries. They are known in English-speaking countries as the Christian Brothers and in the Arab world simply as *al-Frair* (the Frères).

My school had two parts. One was a separate free school consisting of only six elementary classes; it was housed in the same huge building, but it had its own playground, was served by its own team of teachers, and charged no school fees. The other part, the one I was enrolled in, had seven elementary classes and four secondary ones; it had another team of teachers and charged school fees – rather steep ones. It also had a boarding section with a large dormitory, a refectory, and a kitchen, for the use of which it charged student boarders additional fees. Most of the teachers of the free school were Brothers and, therefore, received no salaries; but the school's other expenses were covered by the income from the fee-paying boarding students and day students. However, the annual financial help received from the French Consulate in Jerusalem, though decreasing in recent times, was always welcome to keep the whole institution above water.

For all its foundational relationship with France, my school had only a few French Brothers. The French ones I knew at different stages of my schooling during the nine years (1938-1947) I spent at the Collège des Frères were Frère Pascal, who taught me French language and literature in Secondary One and was the organist at the school's chapel, where I was a member of the choir he directed; Frère Polycarpe, an authoritative old man with white hair, mustache, and a goatee, who was a former director of the school; he taught me bookkeeping and commercial letter writing in Secondary Three and had reputedly been chief of staff of Maréchal Foch in the First World War; Frère René, who did not teach me but was director of the free school; and Frère Sigismond, who did not teach me either and was a member of his staff. Another French Brother, who did not teach at all but was responsible for selling school supplies to students, buying provisions for the boarding school and the Brothers, and collecting students' fees which he went after relentlessly and often ruthlessly by sending defaulting students back home until they paid, was known to us students as Frère Procureur, and his name was Frère Benoît.

Oh yes, there was also Frère Pierre, an old and ever-silent, unassuming, and kind bearded Frenchman who did not teach and whose title was Frère Infirmier, because he took care of the occasional sick students among boarders and the incidental day student in a medical emergency.

The other Brothers at school were of various other nationalities. Brother Cyril, who taught me English, mathematics, and typing in Elementary Seven, was Czechoslovakian. Frère Jean, who taught me French, arithmetic, and catechism in Elementary Four, was Dutch. Brother Xavier was Irish; he taught English language and literature to the highest classes when I was in lower ones, was Irish. Frère Épiphane did not teach me, but he lent me books to read from the school's Arabic library for which he was responsible; he was Lebanese. Frère Alphonse, who was a teacher in the free school and taught my brother André and me to read musical notes in his private time at no charge, was Dutch, and because of him I could then read sheet music to play my banjo that my father had taught me to play by ear, and thus I could be a member of a small band of amateurs that played in town at local occasions. Finally, there was Brother Francis, who taught me English in Secondary One; he was Armenian and, in his capacity as Brother Inspector, he had vast authority in the school and implemented its move to a new system and curriculum leaning more towards an English content. He was the one who steered the curriculum toward making the graduating students able to achieve matriculation in the University of London on passing its public examination in Palestine – this was administered by the British Mandate's Department of Education – as well as to receive the Oxford and Cambridge School Certificate on passing its public examination. He was also the one who lent me the first book on sex I had ever read; it was a book in English, and I think he lent it to other teenage students too, in private and in genuine educational concern and goodness of heart.

The director of the school, the Frère Directeur, was a more distant figure, and his authority was more or less ceremonial, in comparison; he had little to do with the realities of teaching and education. The fact remains that he was, behind the scenes, the final authority at school and, under the superintendence of the regional Frère Visiteur, he made and implemented curriculum policies, bravely attempting to preserve the French content of the curriculum but eventually acceding to an English content that the British Mandate authorities were increasingly pursuing with regard to French educational institutions in Palestine. During my nine years at the Collège des Frères, there were two directors: Frère Octave Laurent, a Frenchman, who was director for eight years; and Frère Imiers Félix, a Lebanese, who followed him and was director in the academic year 1946-47, at the end of which I graduated. Thanks to my London matriculation – I passed the public examination with distinction in 1947 due to my good schooling at the Collège des Frères – I later earned a First Class B.A. (Honours) in Arabic at the University of London in 1964, and a Ph.D. in Arabic literature in 1969 after writing and defending a doctoral dissertation on *Badr Shakir al-Sayyab: His Life and Poetry*.

All these teaching Brothers at the Collège des Frères were not enough to meet the needs of a flourishing school with an excellent reputation, high standards, and coveted accomplishments. The school had to hire lay teachers to help in its educational task, and it usually hired the best qualified persons available, individuals who would be compatible with its ethical, educational, and cultural aims. They were mostly Palestinians but the school also hired others when the need arose.

Of the Palestinians who taught me in the elementary classes, Mr. Bishara Dabbini was my teacher in the Ninth class (upper division) for French, arithmetic, and catechism when I first joined the school and, a few years later, he was to teach me Arabic in Elementary Six. I owe him a great debt of gratitude for giving me a strong foundation in Arabic grammar and for selecting for us students some of the best classical poems of Arabic literature to memorize. Mr. Wadi' Hajjar taught me French and arithmetic in the Eighth class and inculcated the basic rules of computing. Mr. David Ni'metallah, who taught me English in the Eighth class, emphasized correct British pronunciation and spelling, despite the incongruously assigned American textbook, *Tom in England*, which made us students aware of another variety of English. Mr. Musa Salem taught me Arabic in Elementary Four and Elementary Seven, encouraged my imaginative writing and, through his extracurricular interest in the dramatic arts, taught me to act on the stage at school.

Mr. Pierre Sahakian, who taught me French and arithmetic in Elementary Six, emphasized accuracy and meticulous attention to detail; he also taught me catechism, in which I had a one-time notorious difference of religious belief with him, for which he detained me with all my non-Catholic supporters in class till a late evening hour until Brother Inspector intervened and released us. In a spontaneous act of solidarity, the students belonging to the Eastern Orthodox Church, like myself, refused to answer that they were

60

schismatics as the catechism question in the textbook required, and those belonging to the Syriac Orthodox Church similarly refused to answer that, as Jacobites, they were heretics.

Mr. Issa Awad taught me English and geography in Elementary Six; his was the only course on geography in the school's curriculum. And Monsieur Édouard, originally a Turk, taught me French in Elementary Seven with such verve and with such love for the language's wealth of vocabulary and beauty of literary structure that I still retain his enthusiasm for it.

The lay teachers who taught me in the secondary classes included Mr. Mounah Khouri (1918-1996), a Lebanese who taught me Arabic language and literature in Secondary One and Secondary Three and was most elemental in making me love the subject and later become a teacher of it in my adult professional life, first in high schools in Palestine and then at university level in the US and Canada. Since there was no course on Arab history and Islamic civilization ever given at my school, Mr. Khouri's course was the only indirect window on these topics and it was very inspiring, not to mention that he made Arab poets and poetry come alive in his students' minds. After he left Palestine in 1948, he taught at the International College of the American University of Beirut and he continued his own studies there, earning a B.A. and then an M.A. In 1956 he left for the US and obtained a Ph.D. in Arabic literature at Harvard University in 1964. He taught at Georgetown University in Washington, DC, and then joined the University of California at Berkeley where he became Professor of Arabic Literature until he retired in 1989.

After I left Jerusalem in 1968 and emigrated to the US where I became professor of Arabic, I often met Professor Khouri at professional conferences such as the Middle East Studies Association (MESA), and we became very good friends. With his former Berkeley student, Professor Terri L. DeYoung, I edited a Festschrift in his honour entitled *Tradition and Modernity in Arabic Literature* (Fayetteville: University of Arkansas Press, 1997), which he did not live to see. He was a known poet in Arabic, translated and anthologized selections of modern Arabic poetry, and wrote several scholarly books and articles on Arabic literature, in English and Arabic.

Jabra Ibrahim Jabra (1920-1994), born in Bethlehem, taught me English literature in Secondary Three and Secondary Four. Having returned from England, where he earned a B.A. at Fitzwilliam House at Cambridge University in 1943 (and an M.A. in 1948), he taught English literature at the Rashidiyya College in Jerusalem and later, as a part-time teacher, at the Collège des Frères too, where he introduced me to Shakespeare and the Romantic poets, and was destined to have a deep influence on my literary and cultural predilections. His extra-curricular activities included being head of the Arts Club, which he established in 1945 at the Jerusalem YMCA as a venue for public lectures, art exhibits, music recitals, and poetry readings, which I attended regularly to round out my education.

After the *Nakba* of 1948, Mr. Jabra went to Baghdad, where he taught English literature until 1952 at its colleges, then went to Harvard University on a two-year Rockefeller fellowship to study literary criticism. On his return to Baghdad, he headed the publications bureau of the Iraq Petroleum Company and lectured at the College of Arts. In 1977, he was appointed cultural counselor at the Iraqi Ministry of Culture and Information, where he remained until his retirement in 1985. He published three collections of his free verse in Arabic, several Arabic novels and books of literary and art criticism, and became one of the leading modernizing intellectuals in the Arab world. He translated into Arabic over thirty books from Western culture and literature, including seven of Shakespeare's plays, forty of his sonnets, several modern classics such as William Faulkner's *The Sound and the Fury*, and several works of literary and art criticism.

I lost touch with Mr. Jabra after he left Palestine in 1948, but I resumed contact with him after he returned from Harvard to Baghdad in 1954. I met him whenever he returned to Jerusalem and Bethlehem to visit his family during his annual leave; I also visited him in Baghdad in 1967 when I was doing doctoral research on the Iraqi poet Badr Shakir al-Sayyab, and in 1986 and 1988 when I participated in Iraq's international poetry festival of al-Mirbad. I wrote an article on his poetry in an Arabic Festschrift published in 1995 in his honour and edited by his friend, the novelist 'Abd al-Rahman Munif. To further honour him, a street was named after him in Bethlehem.

I translated into English some of his poetry and the two books of his autobiography, *The First Well: A Bethlehem Boyhood* (1995) and *Princesses' Street: Baghdad Memories* (2005). His novels were translated into English by other scholars. In 2001 I published the letters he wrote to me between 1966 and 1994, and in 2002 I published a book in Arabic collecting my previous literary writings on him, *Nafidha 'ala al-Hadatha* (*Window on Modernism*). Among my former teachers, he was the most widely acclaimed person as a literary figure in the Arab world.

There were two Palestinian teachers who taught me history: Mr. Spir Jouzeh in Secondary Three and Mr. Nicola Ziadeh in Secondary Four. They were both excellent in helping me understand the historical developments that led to the prominence of modern-day Europe in the world. The former had a sense of cynicism about Europe's self-concept as the world's cultural centre, the latter a practical approach to the comprehension of motivation and causation associated with historical events. Mr. Ziadeh, with a B.A. (Honours) from the University of London, later earned a Ph.D. in 1950 at the same university and taught history at the American University of Beirut, where he eventually became Chairman of the History Department. He authored several history books and many articles in Arabic and English, and was a consultant to the editors of the Palestinian encyclopedia, *Al-Mawsu'a al-Filistiniyya*. There is a brief entry* on the Collège des Frères in this encyclopedia under *al-Frair* with a mention of graduates who were noted for their later intellectual and literary achievements in Palestine: Anton Lawrence, Diya' al-Din al-Khatib, Issa al-Bandak, Musa Salem Salameh, Musa al-'Alami, Henry Catan and myself. Furthermore, al-Haj Muhammad Amin al-Husseini (later, the Mufti of Palestine) and Shukri al-Harami (later, founder and principal of Al-Umma School) are also said in it to have joined *al-Frair* for some time to learn French.

Of my lay teachers of chemistry, physics, and mathematics in the secondary classes, I have little recollection, not because their courses were not interesting or because they did not teach them well. Mr. Alex Hanania, who also owned and ran a pharmacy near the Church of the Holy Sepulchre, made his chemistry classes quite interesting, especially in lab periods; and so did Mr. Ya'coub Saba in his physics classes; Mr. Zacharia's math classes were the most challenging to me and he seemed the most distant among my teachers.

At the confident suggestion of the Brother Inspector, and in the interest of saving time – and school fees – I skipped Secondary Two in 1945-46 and finished my four-year secondary schooling in only three years. This left gaps in my knowledge, so that my rank, which had always been the first in class, came down to third or so. My performance in the sciences and mathematics suffered most, despite a whole month of supplemental, private tutoring by Mr. Ashkar in the evening, which may explain how little I remember of the teachers who taught me these courses.

But I will not forget two lay teachers who taught me English in the secondary classes. One was Mr. Abraham, an Englishman and a Jew, who taught me English in Secondary One. He walked with a limp, and he also had a speech defect that made spittle fly from his lips when he spoke. He impressed me as being a learned man, and I thought I could learn much from him if only the students in class would allow him to teach, but they made fun of him in many mischievous ways, and his class was never under control. He was so earnest in his desire to teach that he came down from his teacher's platform to the level of the boys in class and often leaned his body on the front desks of the students in the first row as he spoke. His flying spittle hit those students especially, to the amusement of their classmates, who could hardly conceal their snickering. Perhaps in self-defence or more probably in mischief, the students in the front rows daubed the front edges of their desks with chalk before the start of every English period. But in his enthusiasm, Mr. Abraham still leaned his body on the front desks, unwittingly smearing his suit with white chalk, which added to the class's entertainment. In the end, the Brother Inspector dismissed Mr. Abraham, after due compensation, at the end of his first month of teaching and took over the class himself and taught it well. We read *Oliver Twist* by Charles Dickens with him.

The other lay teacher who taught me English was a young Englishman in his mid-twenties, a soldier of the British army in Palestine, whose name has slipped my mind. He was a graduate of the University of London and taught me English in Secondary Four in 1946-47, my last year at the Collège des Frères. Handsome and clean-shaven, he arrived punctually at school in his military uniform and always carried his rifle with him. He leaned his rifle on the wall behind him, sat at his desk on the platform in front of the small class of twelve graduating students, and taught with composure and full control. His particular assignment was to teach composition as well as the writing of *précis*, both being requisites for the University of London matriculation exam. Mr. Jabra's assignment was to teach English literature to the same class at another time, and Mr. Ayyash's to teach English grammar. Between the three of them, the class achieved one of the best results in English the school has ever had in public examinations.

There were also two priests. Father Augustine Marmarji (1881-1963) was Iraqi. He was a member of the Dominican religious order in Jerusalem whose community lived at their monastery with its internationally famous École Biblique et Archéologique on Nablus Road outside the Damascus Gate of the Old City. A well-known and widely published linguist of Semitic languages, he taught me a course on Christianity in Secondary Three. Unlike previous courses of catechism I had taken at school, his was a refreshingly clear and organized view of Christian tenets and ethics, well worthy of his order's founder, St. Dominic (1170-1221), who officially called his order *Fratres Praedicatores*. It is true that Father Augustine's lessons were based on assertive predications, but he intelligently brought them together in a logical system that was fairly acceptable to his students' minds.

Father Jibra'il Abu Sa'da (1907-1965) was a Palestinian born in Beit Sahur, next to Bethlehem. He was the parish priest of the Melchite (or Melkite) church in Jerusalem, the Melchites in the Near East being an Eastern Christian Church in union with Rome since 1724, popularly called Greek Catholic and following the same Byzantine rites as the Greek Orthodox Church. He was later to become bishop and then archbishop as his church grew in Palestine. His course on the history of modern Arabic literature, which I took in my graduating year, was based on some of his published books on the subject and focused on the cultural influences that Europe had had on the development of modern Arabic literature in the nineteenth and early twentieth centuries as well as on the genius of certain Arab writers and poets he liked, such as the Lebanese Fawzi al-Ma'louf (1899-1930) in Brazil about whom he had written a book.

Another priest, who was resident at school for a few years, never taught me, although he taught catechism in some elementary classes. He was an Arab Maronite priest, the Maronites being an ancient Eastern Christian Church based in Lebanon, which has a Syriac liturgy and which has been in union with Rome for several centuries. He was called Father Hanna, and the students addressed him as Abouna Hanna. What I liked about him was his amazing ability to give eloquent and captivating sermons in Arabic on Sunday, when he occasionally officiated in the school chapel. This was rare, because the daily, thirty-minute Mass at the school chapel was usually said in Latin by an Italian or other European priest who came to our school from the nearby Latin Patriarchate of Jerusalem for that purpose and delivered no sermon. One of those European priests was Father Matt, a short Dutchman whose name sounded like the Arabic verb "he died" *(mat)*, which made the students chuckle when addressing him as *abouna mat* (our father died). But he was in fact very much alive, with a ruddy round face, searching blue eyes, and a constant smile. The Catholic students liked him because confession to him at the chapel's confessional in the late afternoon on Saturday was always quick and brief, and the penance imposed on them for whatever sins they confessed to him in preparation for receiving Holy Communion on Sunday morning was always to say Hail Mary three times. I learned this from my Catholic classmate, Dr. Issa Araïche, a well-known dentist, now living in Toronto.

Sunday Mass was memorable when Father Hanna gave one of his inspiring sermons in Arabic. I delighted in his rhetoric and his narrative, conveyed in the classical Arabic language of whose timbre and nuance he was a master. I sincerely appreciated his Christian message, too, for he always ended with a reference to the happy eternal life which, he said, "I hope for you and myself. Amen." The Sunday Mass sung in Latin which was called High Mass in English or Messe Chantée in French, was memorable, too. As a member of the choir, I participated in chanting parts of the Mass under the direction of Frère Pascal, who also played the organ. The choir's part was to respond in Latin to the priest's sung words of the Mass, the longest single part being the singing of the Creed, when the priest sang one sentence at a time and the choir sang the next, and so on. By the time the priest sang "*Ite missa est*," declaring the end of the Mass, more than one hour after the beginning, every one of the students was ready to go out to the playground, particularly the Catholic ones who had fasted in order to receive Holy Communion and now finally had the opportunity to buy and eat breakfast – a crunchy *ka'ka* with sesame seeds, along with an oven-boiled egg, hot falafel, or ground thyme sold to them by the patiently waiting peddlers.

All rituals aside, one of the most touching moments of Catholic devotion I still recall from my schooldays is that of the *Angelus* when, on hearing the school's special tintinnabulation at noon, observant teachers stopped teaching for a few seconds to remember the Incarnation – the union of divinity with humanity in Jesus Christ – in silence with their class. Whenever I see the painting of the nineteenth century French artist Millet, *L'Angélus,* with a peasant woman standing at noon in the field with bent head in a moment's pause of prayer, I remember that exalted moment in class and I admire the way the artist captured it.

As an Orthodox Christian, I do of course share with the Catholics common tenets established in the first millennium of Christianity before the Western and Eastern Churches were separated for doctrinal and administrative political reasons; but as far as I could in my boyhood, I clung to my Orthodoxy, with my parents' guidance, and I attended the Divine Liturgy at the Cathedral of Mar

Ya'coub (St James) near the Church of the Holy Sepulchre, on the Sundays when I had no school, especially during the summer holidays. This cathedral was the main parish church of the Arab Orthodox community of Jerusalem to which my family belonged; its Divine Liturgy was in Arabic, and it was always wholly chanted in accordance with the old Byzantine music of the Eastern Orthodox Church. The Epistle and the Gospel readings were also chanted in Arabic, as were the calls of the priest and the responses of the congregation led by the choir. Much of the Orthodox theology is contained in the Divine Liturgy itself, its hymns and their wording.

Not all Orthodox priests of my parish church gave sermons, but those who did, like Father Nicola Khoury in my schooldays and Father George Khoury later on, gave very good homilies that were simple and quite effective. Confessions of sins to the priest were hardly ever heard in detail, except from those who asked for them. Those who prepared themselves for Holy Communion by fasting approached the priest reverently in one group before Divine Liturgy, and he spread his stole over their heads as he asked them to repent in silence and ask for God's forgiveness, and then he said a prayer of absolution for them all. My parents, my siblings and I received Holy Communion only a few times in the year, mainly at Christmas and Easter, and on certain feast days such as those of the Virgin Mary, St James, St. Peter and St. Paul. Before we could receive Holy Communion, we had to abstain from meat and dairy products for a specific number of days, as well as fasting from food and drink from midnight on the day. Our determination to lead a morally better life was also a requirement.

And so, being a graduate of the Collège des Frères, I grew up to be an Orthodox Christian who knew many aspects of the Catholic faith and its rituals, and who retained an open mind to all religions and other beliefs.

I had a Jewish classmate in Elementary Seven whose seat in class was just next to mine. His name was Solomon Khalifa, and he had an older brother in a higher class. Solomon was a very nice guy and a good friend, his skin was rather dark, and he had pitch-black hair. He was shy and had a feeling that the other students did not like him, and he once told me so, crying; I comforted him and I said I liked him and assured him I was his friend. Originally from Iraq, he spoke Arabic well and was good in all his courses. I think he used to go to the schools of the Alliance Française and wanted to continue his education in French when his family moved from Iraq to Palestine. But he did not stay at the Collège des Frères for more than one academic year, 1943-44.

I also had a Jewish classmate in Secondary Four in 1946-47, my last year at the Collège des Frères. His name was Henry Alfandery. Originally from Hungary, he was fair-complexioned and knew no Arabic. He was a good-natured person, but he was not a special friend of mine, and I did not know him for more than that academic year. One thing I remember well about him was that he absented himself from class on a seemingly regular basis once or twice a month. One day I asked him the reason for this, and he said he went for military training. He did not elaborate, and I did not pursue the subject with him. I thought he must belong to one of the Zionist youth organizations, and I continued to be reserved with him.

That same year, there were two Muslim students in my class of twelve: Rashid Qutub and Mundhir Abdel-Hadi. The former was a meek person with a small build who was very studious. He eventually made a fortune as a businessman in Libya, but all his assets were seized in 1977 when Qaddafi "nationalized" the country's economic resources. The latter student, Mundhir, who sat next to me in class, was a happy-go-lucky person who was tall and handsome, but not very interested in his studies. His father, Rohi Adel-Hadi, had a high position at the secretariat of the British mandatory government housed in the south wing of the King David Hotel, and was one of the few survivors saved from under the rubble several days after it was blown up on 22 July 1946 by members of the Zionist group Irgun*, causing the death of ninety-one innocent persons – Arabs, Jews, and Britons. The last I heard about Mundhir was that he now lives in England.

The remaining members of my graduating class were Christians, and most of them were my friends, but after the 1948 *Nakba* when Palestinians were dispossessed of their homes, dislocated from their country, and dispersed in all directions upon the creation of Israel, I lost contact with them. I later learned about the whereabouts of some, like Fouad Geadah of Haifa, who became a medical doctor and practiced in Beirut for many years until he retired and went to live in Florida. Issa Araïche became a dentist and practiced in Jerusalem and the US; he is now retired in Toronto. Jack Ja"ar of Bethlehem is now a professor of mathematics at the University of Bethlehem. I know nothing about my friends Rohi Bader, Farouk Abdennour, Sami Sfeir, and the others. May our paths come together again when there is peace and justice in Jerusalem and the Holy Land.

VII. AL-NAKBA:
THE 1948 CATASTROPHE OF PALESTINE

In the annals of modern Palestine, no year is burnt into the memory of the Palestinians as deeply and as painfully as 1948. That is the year of the *Nakba*, the catastrophe of being dispossessed by Israel of their livelihood, their homes, and their homeland, the consequences of which have continued to hurt them ever since. Other Arabs and Muslims all over the world have continued to share the loss of the Palestinians and have stood with them in solidarity, along with others whose consciences summoned them to reject this inequity. It is my firm belief that the possibility of peace in the Middle East will not be realized until and unless the injustice that the Palestinians have endured for so many years is acknowledged and then dealt with to their satisfaction in a mutual agreement with their opponents. This state of affairs has continued to fester for too long, and international politics have not so far been able to foster reconciliation or bring peace to the area because of the conflicting interests of the powers that can effectively deliver peace – and their blindness to the reality of the injustice perpetrated.

Many books have been written about what came to be called the Arab-Israeli conflict*, as well as about Zionism and Israel, Arab nationalism and Palestinian identity. I do not wish here to add to the plethora of such books or to enter into historical and political debates supporting one point of view or another. I only want to express my own feelings as I was growing up in Jerusalem, witnessing the events, being unwillingly made into a person without a country, and forced to bear the consequences until this very day.

I was nineteen years old when the *Nakba* occurred. I had graduated from the Collège des Frères on July 1st, 1947 and had been accepted for a British Mandate government job as an accountant of the Department of Prisons at the Central Prison in Jerusalem. At the same time, I had been admitted as a student in the Law School run in Jerusalem by the Law Council of Palestine, and I had regularly begun to attend its evening classes given by British and Palestinian (Arab and Jewish) professors. I was contemplating a career in the legal profession and was full of hope that a good life was ahead of me. This hope was normal and not a presumptuous expectation: I was a human being looking forward to achieving my inalienable right to the pursuit of happiness.

Yet a Palestinian Arab under the British who had, in the Balfour Declaration of 1917, promised to view with favour "the establishment in Palestine of a national home for the Jewish people" was not expected, it seems, to have this inalienable right. A Palestinian Arab whose people lived for centuries in Palestine was not expected, it seems, to live in liberty and to pursue happiness after a nineteenth century Jewish European movement called Zionism, founded by Theodor Herzl (1860-1904), developed political aims to take over his country and succeeded in having the Balfour Declaration's principles and aims incorporated into the League of Nations' charter of the British Mandate for Palestine in 1922.

By the 1940s, the British mandatory government considered that it had fulfilled its mandate in Palestine. It had allowed Jews from Europe and elsewhere to immigrate into the country, buy land, develop businesses and schools, build institutions, and establish a coherent society constituting a "national home." Faced with Palestinian opposition in the 1920s and 1930s including the 1936-39 rebellion and with Zionist terrorism in the late 1930s and the 1940s – including the blowing up of the south wing of the King David Hotel, which housed the British Mandate's secretariat, killing ninety-one civil servants and civilian visitors – it decided to leave Palestine on May 15, 1948 and let the newly established United Nations Organization decide the fate of the country.

When I graduated from high school in 1947, the political atmosphere in Palestine was tense. It gradually deteriorated into violent acts committed by Zionist and Palestinian groups. The British were increasingly losing control. I was aware, on the whole, that the Palestinian leadership was in disarray. Other than negativism, I observed that its politicians did not have well-planned policies vis-à-vis the British or the United Nations. Its military activities lacked coordination and dependable weapon supplies. The seven states of the newly formed Arab League, which were supposed to help the Palestinians, were not in a better condition.

I was aware, too, that the Jewish political leadership was organized and had clear-cut goals. Its military activities had strategic aims, were well supplied with weapons by international Jewish organizations and friendly Western countries, and used all possible tactics to achieve their ends, including terrorizing the Arab civilian population and causing them – sometimes compelling them – to evacuate their homes and abandon their lands and properties.

In September 1947, the United Nations Special Committee on Palestine issued its report. A majority of its members proposed to partition Palestine into an Arab state and a Jewish state, and to internationalize an enclave comprising Jerusalem, Bethlehem, and the nearby villages. A minority of its members proposed a federated state for the whole of Palestine with areas of Jewish communal autonomy. On November 29, 1947, the United Nations General Assembly adopted the Committee's majority report, with minor amendments, by a vote of thirty-three to thirteen, with ten abstentions; there were fifty-six members in all. The delegations of the Arab member states who had voted against the resolution in the United Nations General Assembly walked out. Their position was that the United Nations Organization had no authority to partition a country against the will of the majority of its people.

The Partition Plan voted for by thirty-three countries of the United Nations was a triumph for the Zionists. I remember the jubilation of the Jews in the streets of Jerusalem on this occasion, particularly Ben Yehuda Street and Jaffa Road, where Jewish people sang and danced publicly, and wine was offered free to everyone until a late hour. Arab anger intensified, and a three-day strike in Palestine was declared on December 2nd protesting the United Nations resolution. On the first day of the strike, one of the Jewish police sergeants of the prison where I worked arrived late to the office at the Central Prison in Jerusalem with a bloody head and face, having been bludgeoned by an Arab mob as he made his way to work. The Jews and the Arabs in Palestine were at daggers drawn, and a sort of civil war was at hand.

The British attempt to control Jerusalem by dividing it into different zones, with restricted movement from one to the other and with checkpoints between them manned by police, was not successful in restraining the opponents, each of whom was attempting to dominate as much of the city and the country as possible before the British withdrew. The Jewish military groups prepared themselves, and on November 30th the Haganah called up all Jews in Palestine between the ages of seventeen and twenty-five to register for military service; the Haganah also succeeded in obtaining arms from Czechoslovakia to support its Plan Gimmel, which aimed to destabilize the Palestinian population and occupy strategic positions in Jerusalem and other locations in Palestine. The Irgun attacked Arab residential areas in Jerusalem, Jaffa, and Haifa; and Palestinians were killed at Herod's Gate in Jerusalem, at Haifa's oil refinery, and elsewhere. The Haganah blew up the Semiramis Hotel in the Jerusalem residential area of Qatamon, killing twenty civilians. As a passerby, I miraculously escaped from dying in an explosion set by the Irgun in the area outside of Jaffa Gate on January 7, 1948, in which twenty-five Palestinian civilians were killed and many were injured. Like all Palestinian Arabs, I was a victim of events and of the decisions being made by those in authority.

On December 8, 1947, Britain officially announced its intention to the United Nations to terminate its mandate over Palestine on May 15, 1948. The remaining months of the British Mandate were punctuated by daily acts of violence in Jerusalem and all over Palestine. In January, the Palestinian guerrilla commander 'Abd al-Qadir al-Husseini secretly returned to Jerusalem from his ten-year exile to organize military actions; and Fawzi al-Qawuqji, the Lebanese guerrilla leader from Tripoli, entered Palestine with a small Arab volunteer force called *Jaysh al-Inqadh* (The Rescue Army), sanctioned by the Arab League.

One of the spectacular events brought about by Palestinian Arab irregulars was the blowing up of the offices of the Jewish-owned newspaper *Palestine Post* on a side street off Jaffa Road on February 1, 1948, killing twenty Jewish civilians. The main participant in this event was an unsuspected but spunky Arab colleague of mine at the office of the Central Prison named Khalil Janho; he had succeeded in passing the checkpoint and entering the Jewish restricted zone wearing a British police uniform and driving a police truck carrying the explosives. He boasted of his daring act to his colleagues in the office on the next day and explained that his escape route after the explosion was on foot across the historic Muslim cemetery of Mamillah.

This same Khalil Janho had approached me a couple of months earlier to inveigle me into participating in a scheme whereby he and others would arrange to attack the police armoured car in which, as the prison's accountant, I would be transported from Barclays Bank with a satchel chained to my wrist containing the sum of about 10,000 Palestine pounds (about $35,000 US) in cash, representing the salaries of the Central Prison's Arab and Jewish policemen. Despite the atmosphere of lawlessness and the increasing loss of government control, I refused to have anything to do with his scheme, preferring to do my official duty and pay the policemen their deserved salaries as I did at the end of every month in the presence of Major McGee, the British director of the Central Prison. He would empty on his desk the envelope I had prepared, containing the policeman's salary in pounds, shillings, piasters, and mils; and the policeman, having signed against his name on my pay-sheet, would salute the Major, collect his salary, salute again saying, "Thank you, Sir," and walk out to be followed by another policeman in the alphabetical order of his name that I listed on the pay-sheet. The salary sometimes included an expected increment because of a rank promotion, a new marriage, the birth of a new child, or an officially announced change in the cost of living, for each of which there was a specific allowance added to his basic salary that I would have calculated from the exact date of the change in his status to the end of the month. How could I dare deprive such a policeman of his due salary. I could not.

Another spectacular event brought about by Palestinian Arab irregulars was the blowing up of buildings and shops on Ben Yehuda Street in Jerusalem on February 22, 1948 killing fifty-seven Jewish civilians, injuring dozens, and reducing to rubble one of the busiest Jewish commercial centres of the modern city. This was followed on March 11th by the blowing up of the Jewish Agency on King George V Avenue, killing twelve and injuring over eighty Jewish civilians; the Jewish Agency was the overarching Zionist organization in Palestine, almost "a state within a state," headquarters of the Haganah and of the Zionist political and cultural institutions of Palestine, in touch with the World Zionist Organization and other international Jewish bodies for financial and other support.

By this time, I had decided to leave the service of the British

Mandate government, so I resigned and began in March 1948 to work as an accountant in the Accounts Department of Barclays Bank in Jerusalem. I thought that, since my position in the Palestine civil service would end on May 15, 1948, with the end of the British Mandate, a position in a commercial bank like Barclays would be more secure. I liked my new work and enjoyed having new colleagues and a congenial workplace. The former Jewish employees of the bank had been assigned to work in a new branch of Barclays in the Jewish sector of Jerusalem to serve Jewish clients who were unwilling to risk coming to the bank in the Arab sector for their business transactions.

The general situation in the country was becoming very dangerous as the Palestinian and Jewish groups faced each other in battles all over the country despite international attempts calling for a truce. There was a big battle west of Jerusalem, over the Arab village of Castal – on a hill dominating the main road westward sloping down to the Mediterranean – that threatened to cut off the Jewish western part of Jerusalem from Tel Aviv. The village changed hands several times during the battle but finally the Haganah succeeded in retaking it on April 9, 1948 and in killing 'Abd al-Qadir al-Husseini. Three miles away from the village, the Irgun and the Stern Gang attacked the Arab village of Deir Yassin that same day, massacring some two hundred and forty-five of its inhabitants and parading the survivors in open trucks in the streets of Jerusalem next day to instill fear in the hearts of the Arabs.

The death of 'Abd al-Qadir al-Husseini was a great blow to the Arab fighters and the Palestinian population. He was given a big funeral at al-Haram al-Sharif attended by thousands of Arabs. The Arab employees of Barclays Bank who could not attend sent wreaths of flowers, and a bank colleague of mine, Miss Sonia Toubbeh, was the one who took up a collection from the Arab employees for this purpose. A good organizer, she also collected money from the employees every month for their ten o'clock coffee, which was served daily by the bank's messenger at every employee's table.

The Arabs were losing ground. After some initial successes in the north of Palestine, Fawzi al-Qawuqji and his Rescue Army withdrew from the Jewish settlement of Mishmar Ha'emek on April 13, 1948. That same day, Palestinian irregulars in Jerusalem ambushed a Jewish convoy taking supplies to the besieged Hebrew University on Mount Scopus in the Arab sector of Jerusalem, and the fight with its Haganah escorts resulted in the death of thirty-nine Jews and six Palestinians. The British successively withdrew from major cities like Tiberias and Haifa, and the Haganah captured them, causing their Arab inhabitants to flee. By the end of April, Jaffa was surrounded by the Haganah and the Irgun, and most of the city's Arab inhabitants were forced to flee by sea to Gaza and Egypt. Similarly, Palestinian residential areas in the modern Arab sector of Jerusalem like Qatamon, Talibiyya, the German Colony, the Greek Colony, Upper Baq'a and Lower Baq'a were occupied by the Haganah in Operation Jebusi*, and many of their Arab inhabitants were driven out or had already fled to Bethlehem, Ramallah, or across the Jordan river to Amman. My uncles and aunts on the Atallah side of my family living in Upper Baq'a became refugees in Bethlehem, except for my aunt Melia, her husband Lutfi Atallah, and their three daughters who had already fled to Cairo where they were neighbours of the well-known Palestinian educator and writer, Khalil Sakakini, and his two daughters who had fled from Qatamon. All these civilian Arabs fleeing for their lives abandoned their homes and properties to the advancing Jewish forces.

My evening classes at the Law School were interrupted, and the school itself was eventually closed because neither its professors nor its students could reach it safely with the continuous fighting and the unstable situation in the country. Legally speaking, the British continued to be the authority in the land, and their flag continued to fly over official buildings, including the British High Commissioner's residence and office on a remote mountain south of Jerusalem, but their actual control of the country was becoming less and less effective by the day. Palestine was descending into a state of chaos, with Jewish and Arab armed groups controlling different areas.

On April 30, 1948, Barclays Bank paid its employees their salaries plus a two-month salary advance, announcing to them that it would call them back to resume their duties when conditions of business became viable. This turned out to be a severance pay for me and for most of the lower rank employees; those in higher ranks were offered a transfer to branches of Barclays Bank in Cyprus, Ethiopia, or other nearby countries if they wanted to remain in the employ of the bank. For me, it meant an unpaid period of idleness that would last well into the fall of 1949, a period during which I saw the *Nakba* eat away at my country, destroy the fabric of my society, and disperse my people in different directions as Israel rose to become a new nation, a Jewish state, immediately recognized by the US and other countries, while the truncated remnants of Palestine languished in disarray.

As the *Nakba* was unfolding and wreaking havoc in Palestine, I was living with my parents and siblings in our home in the Old City of Jerusalem, in the neighbourhood inside the city walls at Jaffa Gate. The Jewish Quarter of the Old City, a mile to the south-east, with about seventeen hundred Jewish residents and about two hundred defenders, was besieged by Palestinian forces. Jewish fighters in the new city tried unsuccessfully to break through Jaffa Gate and Nabi Dawood (Zion) Gate to help them. The battle was persistent, and fighting was almost continuous for the two weeks before the end of the British Mandate. The Haganah fighters in the Jewish Quarter, assisted by a few members of the Irgun and Stern Gang, resisted defiantly, and the other Jewish fighters outside the city walls made repeated but unsuccessful attempts to break the siege.

The Palestinian armed men on the city wall drove back all Jewish attackers coming in successive desperate droves from the new city, and those in the alleys of the Old City surrounding the Jewish Quarter kept their ground and made inroads into it by blowing up some Jewish structures. My family and I took shelter in the windowless room on the first floor of our house one night when the fighting was at its worst; we could hear the Hebrew shouts of the attackers outside Jaffa Gate encouraging one another to advance, and we winced at the explosions of mortar projectiles hurled by them as they shelled our neighbourhood. The next day, we found out that one mortar shell had hit the big dome of the Holy Sepulchre, causing a fire, that several persons were injured and killed in their homes, and that many dead bodies of Jewish attackers were strewn in the open area outside Jaffa Gate – and that the Old City of Jerusalem remained in Palestinian hands.

On April 30, 1948, the Arab League states met in Amman to assess the situation in Palestine, and their meeting was attended for the first time by the chiefs of staffs of the Arab armies. The latter advised that six divisions and air squadrons were the minimum force required to counter the Haganah, but the Arab political leaders refused to believe that that much was necessary. Less than half of this force was sent into Palestine on May 15th, when the British Mandate actually ended, and all it could do was to hold some of the Palestinian Arab territories already in the hands of the Palestinian fighters, including the Old City of Jerusalem*, but it ceded Ramleh and Lydda, and other Arab locations, causing Palestinian inhabitants to flee. The civilian Palestinian population was demoralized, and thousands fled from the advancing Jewish forces and left the Negev for Gaza and the northern Galilee for Lebanon, some by

Jewish expulsion orders. In the end, more than one million Palestinians sought refuge outside of Palestine. The United Nations Relief and Works Agency (UNRWA) that was created to assist the Palestinians living in camps in the West Bank, the Gaza Strip, Jordan, Lebanon, and Syria provided an initial number of 914,000 refugees in 1950.

There were thousands of other Palestinians who lost their livelihood, their homes, and their lands and properties, who did not live in camps. They managed to live on their own wherever they took refuge and were allowed to work and earn their living. Many of them started new careers and businesses, but they always remembered with pain what they had left behind in Palestine that had been seized by the Jewish forces who created the new state of Israel. Some of these Palestinians were members of my own extended family.

To name a few of them, let me mention the family of my father's sister Olga, whose husband Shihadeh 'Azzouni owned a beautiful red stone house in Ramleh where he and his family lived; he also owned vast orange groves that exported Jaffa oranges to Europe and elsewhere. As a boy, I often used to spend a few days of my summer vacation in Ramleh with my cousins and go to one or the other of their orange groves for good times with them. My aunt Olga's family, forced in 1948 to leave their home in Ramleh and abandon all their orange groves, ended as refugees in Amman. She, her husband, and her grown children started a new life there, and two of their sons, my cousins Edmond and Baheej 'Azzouni, emigrated to the US.

My uncle Ya'coub Atallah, head of the Land Registration Department, lived in Upper Baq'a in Jerusalem with his family. He owned a villa which he and his family had to leave in 1948, along with his brother, my uncle Yousef Atallah and his family, who lived nearby. They all took refuge in Bethlehem and lived in humble apartments rented from the Canawati family near the Church of the Nativity. When a truce was declared in Palestine, my uncle Ya'coub and his family moved to live in a rented apartment in Ramallah, situated in the rump of Palestine that came to be called "the West Bank." He was not allowed by Israel to return to his home in Upper Baq'a; the Israeli government did not allow any refugee to return to his home; my uncle's grown-up children eventually migrated to Amman and the US. My uncle Yousef and his family remained in Bethlehem. His three grown-up sons migrated to Canada and the US; one of them, his eldest son Basem, died in September 2009 in North Carolina, and his ashes were taken to be buried in Bethlehem in fulfillment of his wishes.

My mother's cousin George 'Akra, a goldsmith and jeweler, lived with his wife Nellie and their children in Upper Baq'a in Jerusalem. He and his family had to leave their home in 1948 during the fighting and went to Egypt. Then they returned and took refuge in Ramallah for a while; later on, George built a new stone home for himself and his family in Jerusalem, in the Shu'fat neighbourhood. He continued his work in new premises on Saladin Street in the Arab commercial sector of Jerusalem, helped by his son, Khalil. He owned property on Jaffa Road consisting of a three-story stone building with several apartments and with shops on the ground-floor, located in the Jewish sector of Jerusalem near Cinema Zion; but when Jerusalem was "unified" by Israel on June 28, 1967, and he became a holder of an Israeli ID card like all Palestinians in East Jerusalem, he was not permitted to take possession of his property on Jaffa Road which he had not been able to reach since 1948; it has continued to be held by the Israeli Custodian of Absentee Property.

My mother's cousin Anton Atallah, a judge in the district courts of Jerusalem and Haifa (1939-43) and deputy mayor of Jerusalem (1944-46), lived with his family on Bethlehem Road in Upper Baq'a in Jerusalem. He and his family had to abandon their villa in

1948 to flee the scene of fighting. They lived at one time in the east part of the Arab sector of Jerusalem and then in Amman, where he became Minister of Foreign Affairs for Jordan (1963-67) and head of the Arab Land Bank. His son Anwar migrated to the US.

All these members of my extended family and others suffered as a result of the *Nakba*. Some have died since 1948, but their children and grandchildren continue to suffer like them and remember. Thousands of other Palestinians like my extended family and their descendants were victims of the 1948 events leading to the establishment of Israel, and they lost their livelihoods, their homes, and their lands and properties – even if they could heroically rebuild their lives elsewhere. They all expect justice to be done to them. There are many more thousands of Palestinians who continue to languish in refugee camps, who may or may not have owned land in Palestine and who still wish to return to their original homes in their hometowns and villages, from which they were forcibly evicted or from which they had to flee fearing for their lives. They suffer and remember too. And there are still more thousands who own no land and, like me, have not even lost their homes. Yet they feel the injustice resulting from the *Nakba* as strongly and as deeply as all the other Palestinians because, like them, they have lost the dignity of having a country of their own, of being citizens of their own state, and of living a life of free human beings with all the inalienable rights that ought to be theirs. They all suffer and remember.

The impact of the *Nakba* has been traumatic, and its disastrous results affected every Palestinian living through its unfolding cataclysmic events in 1948 after years of prejudiced British rule fostering Zionist predominance. Its results have also affected all future generations of Palestinians, whether still living in their former homeland or elsewhere under whatever circumstances. The injustice they suffered and continue to remember has to be removed before peace may have a chance.

In short, whether the Palestinians lost their livelihoods, their homes, their lands and properties in 1948 or not, they have inherent rights to their country which was theirs for generations and in which they lived for centuries under varying rules and conditions; and if they have left it, for whatever reason, they continue to have intrinsic human rights recognized by international law to return to it whether they left it willingly, forcibly, or advisedly; and if they choose not to return to it, when a settlement with the opponents is made, they ought to be justly compensated for all their losses.

NOTES

Preface See "Jerusalem: The Archaeology of Memory," *Jusoor,* 9-10 (1998): 35-44; "Books and I," *Banipal,* 29 (Summer 2007): 34-42; and "My First School and Childhood Home," *Jerusalem Quarterly,* 37 (Spring 2009): 27-44.

p. 40. General Edmund Lord Allenby (1861-1936) was the British Commander-in-chief of the Egyptian Expeditionary Force that fought the Ottoman Turks in Palestine in the First World War. He entered Jerusalem, December 9, 1917, and finally defeated the Ottoman Turks at Megiddo in 1918.

p. 56. Information about the date of the establishment of Collège des Frères in Jerusalem was partly supplied by Mr. William Alonzo, President of the Frères Alumni Association in Jerusalem, of which I was one of the founders in 1961. Mr. Alonzo had access to the school's archives. I am further indebted to Mr. Alonzo and his brother, Frère Albert, for information about the financial contribution of the French Consulate.

p. 64. The encyclopedia entry in question is in *Al-Mawsu'a al-Filis-tiniyya , Al-Qism al-'Amm,* ed. Anis Sayegh et al. (Damascus-Beirut, 1984), vol. 3, p. 454.

p. 71. Irgun Zvai Leumi (National Military Organization) was a Zionist group that parented the Stern Gang of Jewish terrorists.

p. 72. For details of works on the conflict, see in *Encyclopedia of the Israeli-Palestinian Conflict,* ed. Cheryl A. Rubenberg, 3 vols. (Boulder/London: Lynne Rienner Publishers, 2010).

p. 79. Operation Jebusi. Jebus (Yebus) is the ancient name of Jerusalem inhabited for many centuries by the Jebusites, a Canaanite tribe, when the city was conquered by the Hebrews.

p. 81. The Jewish Quarter in the Old City surrendered on May 28, 1948 to Major Abd Allah Tell of the Arab Legion of Transjordan, its able-bodied men were taken prisoner, and its civilian residents (women, children, and the aged) were given safe passage through Nabi Dawood (Zion) Gate to the New City.